COASTAL WALKING

COASTAL WALKING

70 great walks around the British Isles

B⬚XTREE

in association with

Country Walking magazine

First published in Great Britain in 1996 by Boxtree Limited

Coastal Walking copyright © Emap Pursuit Publishing 1996

10 9 8 7 6 5 4 3 2 1

Printed and bound in Spain by Gráficas Estella, S.A.

Boxtree Limited
Broadwall House
21 Broadwall
London   SE1 9PL

A CIP catalogue entry for this book is available from the British Library.

ISBN 0 7522 1069 6

Front cover photograph by Lee Frost
Back cover photograph by Derek Forss

The symbols below are used for the route maps you will find with all of the walks.

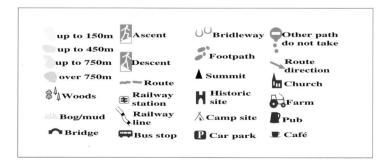

All walks in this book were checked at the time of going to press. Neither the contributors, *Country Walking* magazine, nor Boxtree Limited can accept responsibility for errors owing to changes made since then.

CONTENTS

EDITOR'S NOTE

Welcome to the second *Country Walking* book, featuring walks specially chosen from 'Down Your Way', our monthly guide to routes all over the British Isles.

Country Walking is Britain's best-loved walking magazine and we're delighted to be working with Boxtree Ltd again to present this beautiful book of 70 coastal walks, selected from 'Down Your Way' over the last 20 months. We know our readers love the cliffs and rugged coastal paths of the British Isles and hope, if you're not already a regular reader of *Country Walking* magazine, that you'll enjoy exploring these trails with us.

Our coastline offers a tremendous variety of scenery and a wealth of bird and plant life, just waiting to be discovered. This book will help you do just that. 'Down Your Way' has been around as long as the magazine - since spring 1987 - and is the most popular section, with 27 original walks every month. Distances range from five to fifteen miles and each walk contains a detailed route description, as well as a panel of highlights to look out for along the way, a fact file of essential information, plus a location map and easy-to-follow colour route map. The routes are written and checked by local experts, so it's like having your own personal guide at your side. Just choose the area you'd like to explore (the book is planned from north to south, starting in Scotland and ending in the south west, stopping off in Wales and Ireland on the way.) The index of nearest towns will help you to pinpoint your starting place and the fact files to choose a walk that suits your abilities.

Don't forget to take the relevant Ordnance Survey or Harveys map with you to keep you on the right track.

I do hope you enjoy planning your days out with the help of this lavishly produced book - together we can rediscover the delights of island walking.

Lynne Maxwell
Editor, *Country Walking* magazine.

SCOTLAND

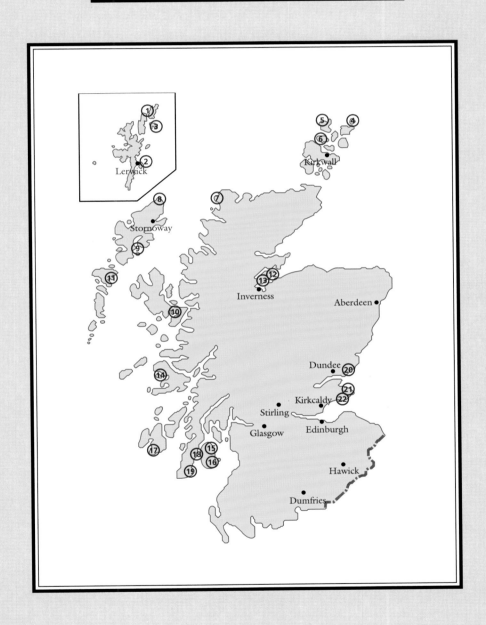

NATURE'S CLOWNS AND PIRATES

Walk over remote moorland and along dramatic cliffs up to 558ft high. There are many opportunities to see the vast numbers of seabirds that nest here, including the famous Albert the albatross.

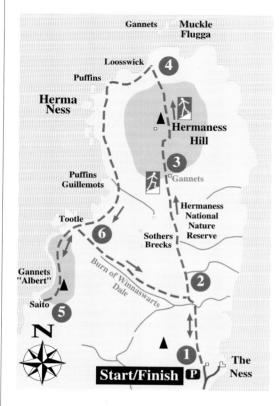

1 From the car park, pass through two kissing gates and follow a clear track through heather. Soon waymarker posts, topped with green paint, guide you on your way.

2 At the Burn of Winnaswarts the track bears left through a sheltered hollow. Climb the slope out of the hollow to where the path divides. Here follow the waymarked posts north, to continue in the same general direction, and cross some duckboards over peat hags. Look left to see a small lochan where three or four dozen Great skuas gather. The skuas breed over the entire moor. They are proud parents and defend their chicks by dive-bombing any human who comes too near, though they rarely make a direct hit. To deter them, hold a stick above your head or wave your arm. Do not stray from the path as the area around it is very boggy.

3 Begin the steady ascent of Hermaness Hill. Beyond, the waymarks take you down towards the edge of the steep seaward-facing slopes. Take care here – it's easy to slide. You can see Muckle Flugga lighthouse from here, and close by some rocks, completely white with droppings and covered with nesting gannets. At your feet the cliffs are dotted with puffin burrows.

4 Turn left to stroll along the edge of the cliffs. Look for rows of guillemots, all facing into the cliff, and fulmars on their nests among the thrift. Descend the slope to East Sothers Dale and look inland to see a stone sheep pen. Cross the stream and climb up the slope. Here look for razorbills and more guillemots. Continue until you come to a waymark.

5 Carry straight on until you can see a huge sheer-sided cliff, covered with hundreds of gannets. You are likely to see a large gull-like bird with dark grey wings and a large hooked beak – Albert. It is a confused black-browed albatross, native to regions nearer the Arctic. It first visited Hermaness in 1970 and may be 30 years old. Sometimes it thinks it is a fulmar and tries to mate with one.

6 Return to the waymark and follow the clear path until you reach the division of the paths in the hollow close to the Burn of Winnaswarts. From here walk back to your car.

ALONG THE WAY

Hermaness, which was declared a nature reserve in 1955, is now managed by Scottish Natural Heritage. During the summer 25,000 puffins, the clowns of the bird world, breed in burrows on the cliff edges. Sixty per cent of the world's population of great skuas nest on the island of Unst; they are pirates, ambushing other birds and forcing them to drop their latest meal. Five per cent of the West European population of gannets breed from April to September on the cliffs of the Hermaness peninsula, turning dark rocks white with their guano. Access is unrestricted, but you are asked not to disturb breeding birds and to tread carefully.

FACT FILE

Distance 6 miles
Time 3–4 hours
Map OS Landranger 1
Start/parking Car park at entrance to nature reserve, grid ref 612149
Terrain Can be wet walking over moorland. Cliffs are sheer, so walk with care. The weather is very changeable; fog, wind, rain, and hot sunshine can all occur at very short notice. Sturdy footwear and warm clothing are essential
Nearest town Lerwick on mainland
Refreshments Baltasound Hotel, Baltasound, Unst
Public transport Fly from Tingwall or Sumburgh on mainland via Loganair, tel 0159 584246. Land at Baltasound airport, return next day. Passenger ferry from Gutcher on the island

of Yell, tel 0195 782259. Crossing takes 10 minutes and the boats run every ½ hour every day. Drive to the north end of the island along the A968. Coach from Lerwick, tel 01595 3162. Bear in mind that you can't return same day, so you need your own transport or somewhere to stay
Stiles None
Not suitable for Young children and dogs. Older children should be aware of the dangers of cliff tops

BIRD ISLAND

A remote Scottish island, reached by an exciting crossing, provides the scene for a great adventure.

1 Walk east from Gungstie around the lovely sandy bay of Nesti Voe. Strike diagonally right towards the hill dyke and go on to the ladder stile over the wall. Follow the low cliffs. Pass through the old wall and the remnants of a building.

2 Begin the steady climb upwards, with the remains of an old wall running along the edge of the cliffs. It was built in the 19th century by Robert Morrison – it took him two years to build and he was paid seven old pence a fathom (6ft). Before then the children of the island kept the cattle from straying too close to the dangerous edges.

3 Continue round the Point of Hovie. Go on climbing to pass Cradle Holm. Near here you should see your first puffin. Walk up past Charlie's Holm towards the great gannetry on Rumble Wick and The Noup. Stay with the wall to reach the trig point on The Noup (700ft). From here you can see Unst, Fetlar, Yell, Whalsay, Bressay and the mainland.

4 Begin the gradual but unrelenting descent to pass several dramatic geos (rocky inlets). Follow the footpath sign that takes you away from another sheer geo. Continue along North Croo. Climb the ladder stile and follow the wall, keeping north of the Hill of Papilgeo. Cross the hill dyke to pick up your outward path.

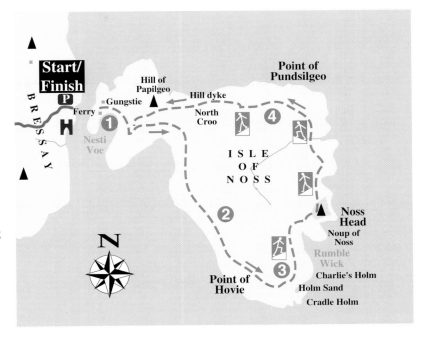

FACT FILE

Distance 5 miles
Time 3 hours
Map OS Landranger 4
Start/parking A frequent, regular and inexpensive car ferry leaves Albert Building in the centre of Lerwick. It takes 5 minutes to cross the sound to Maryfield on the Isle of Bressay. Drive across the island, following signposted directions for Noss (3 miles). Park at the top of the last hill and walk down the track to the jetty, grid ref 528411
Terrain Easy walking, but steep climbs. Immense care is required on the cliffs
Nearest town Lerwick
Refreshments None on the island unless the wardens have time to make a cup of tea
Public transport An inflatable dinghy to Noss is operated by SNH. A small charge is made for the return journey. The island can be visited from mid-May until mid-August, but not on Mondays and Thursdays. Wait at the jetty for the dinghy. If the sea is too rough a red flag is flown. Check with the Tourist Information Centre in Lerwick before you set off for Noss, tel 01856 875807
Stiles Two, easy
Suitable for Children. No dogs

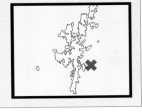

ALONG THE WAY

This dramatic and challenging walk around the island of Noss is great fun, particularly if you are interested in birds. You will see up to 100,000 of them, pecking and preening.
The island is owned by the Garth Estate and is jointly managed by Scottish Natural Heritage. It is home to 400 Shetland ewes and during lambing season these are brought inside the hill dyke to avoid disturbing the breeding of great skuas. The rocks of the island are old red sandstone. As the horizontal layers weathered, innumerable ledges were created, just right for this huge population of birds to nest close to their feeding grounds. Cradle Holm (600ft) is a grassy-topped stack where once a 'cradle' on two cables carried shepherds and their sheep across. Others used the cradle to collect eggs and feathers. The contraption was removed in 1864. Today the stack is a haven for guillemots, razorbills and great black-backed gulls.

Magnificent views can be had from Noss Head

DOUBLE ADVENTURE

Getting to and from Fetlar is an adventure in itself. The walk, which takes you over rough pasture, along dramatic cliffs, around the Inner Brough and beside an RSPB bird hide, makes it a doubly exciting day.

1 From the sheep pen, walk back to take a track on your right through heather moorland. Pass through a gate and walk towards the deserted farm of Still. Take the gate on the right before the farm and turn left, maintaining the same general direction. Beyond the next gate in the fence ahead, continue along a sheep trod towards the sea. While still ¼ mile from the bay, walk left to see a ruined roundhouse.

2 Continue to the beach and walk right. Carry on, with care, along the steadily climbing cliffs, outside the fence. Cross several tiny streams that hurry over the cliff edge and walk round the end of sturdy walls. Pass the roofless Smithfield House at Strand and go on round the end of two more walls. Look for a ruined watermill on a small stream. Pass a gated plantiecrub (a walled enclosure for growing cabbages). Be alert as you walk along this section for the many narrow, deep geos (chasms into which the sea flows).

3 Walk round the rock-strewn headland of Hesta Ness and continue around Skarpi Geo, where you might spot the remains of winding gear used in quarrying. Pass several more narrow precipitous geos that expose faces of conglomerate rock, some of the best in the country – look for natural arches, caves and stacks. Walk over the turf as you climb the south-facing slope of Strandburgh. Head for a small building at the top of the slope and pass through its ruined walls on to the promontory of Inner Brough.

4 Walk ahead over the grassy top, through vast patches of thrift. Pause to view the isle of Outer Brough, to which there is no access. Between the two Broughs lies the narrow Brough Sound, far below. Leave Inner Brough and cross a wet pasture towards a fence which continues uphill. Keep to the right of the fence, with heather moorland stretching away on both sides. At the brow you can glimpse Everland farmhouse; head in that direction by crossing the fence. Keep to the right of a large area of reedy pools. Step through a ruined grassy wall and then over two more fences. Then walk beside a wall at the back of Smithfield, another wet area.

5 Take the left of two gates beyond the house and strike over the pasture to Everland farmhouse to join a track and then a metalled road. Continue to the settlement of Funzie (pronounced Finnie). Bear right and walk to the start of Loch Funzie. Walk left up the wide grassy track that climbs through heather to the disused coastguard look-out station. Cross right to the fence and then left, down the slope, over grass and heather, to the edge of the Geo of Litlaland. Carry on left

along the cliffs, where you can see the deformed conglomerate rock, dramatically exposed. Take care round Staves Geo.

6 Head inland to see Croo Water and then carefully return to the cliff edge of the Snap. Go on round the promontory of Butsa to join a narrow path that takes you over the turf to a fence. Follow this path down until you reach the RSPB hide. Here you might see red-throated divers and the rare red-necked phalaropes.

7 Follow the waymarks to return to the road. Turn left and walk on to rejoin your car.

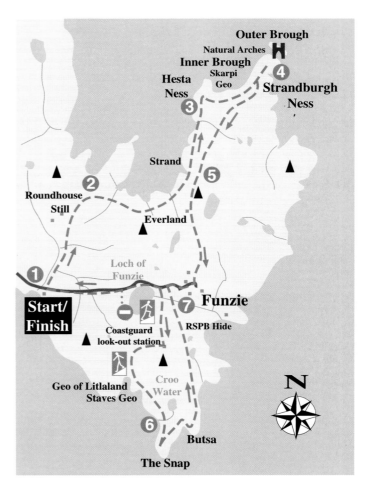

ALONG THE WAY

Fetlar lies south of the Island of Unst and measures about 5 miles by 2½ miles. It is a green island with very little peat. The grass provides rich grazing for sheep.

To the left of Outer Brough you can glimpse a remnant of a stone wall. Here, it is believed, was a Norse monastic settlement. Today many large black-backed gulls sit and preen on large patches of scurvygrass.

SHETLAND

FACT FILE

Distance 9½ miles
Time 5–6 hours
Map OS Landranger 1
Start Leave the pier by the only road and drive along the B9088 to pass through Houbie. Ignore the left turn to Aith and drive to the top of the hill, grid ref 643900
Parking Top of hill, east of Aith, on a verge close to a large sheep pen built of concrete blocks
Terrain Easy walking but watch out for the wet areas
Nearest town Lerwick on mainland
Refreshments None on route. At Interpretative Centre and also small tea room at Houbie. Interpretative Centre open Wednesday, Thursday, Saturday and Sunday
Public transport The roll on-roll off Fetlar ferry takes 25 minutes from Gutcher on Yell to Oddsta. You will need to book in advance. For more information on all inter-island services, tel 01426 986763
Stiles None
Suitable for Older children and dogs (on leads at times)

Divert slightly inland from the route near point 6 to see Croo Water

NORTHERN DELIGHTS

North Ronaldsay is further north than the southern tip of Norway and is the most remote of Orkney's north isles. This walk takes you along its shores and its narrow roads, where you will feel that you have stepped back into a time when old traditions still prevailed.

1 Turn right out of the airfield and walk to the war memorial. Turn left here and head along the narrow road for 2 miles. Ahead, across Dennis Loch, you can see the old lighthouse, which was built in 1789. It was, however, unsatisfactory and the light was taken to Start Point on Sanday. It was replaced by the ball of masonry that you can still see today.

2 Continue round the sharp bend to the new lighthouse. If you have timed your visit right you can be taken to the top at the discretion of the principal keeper.

3 Return along the road until you approach the shore near Snash Ness. Here you may want to step outside the drystone sheep dyke and continue south along Linklet Bay to Bride's Ness; if you feel you are short of time, return along the road to turn left at the war memorial and then left again at the crossroads to walk to Bride's Ness. As you near the shore, look left to see part of an old turf and stone dyke, called Muckle Gersty. It is one of two that divided the island into three and both could be pre-Norse. Legend has it that they were erected by three brothers to apportion the island.

4 Pass through the gate in the dyke to the beach and bear right to pass the fishermen's tall cairn topped with an old bell. Walk on along the rough shore to another gate in the sheep dyke. This gives access to the Brock of Burrian, part of an extensive Iron Age settlement. Continue along the silvery sands of Nouster Bay to a gate on to a road. To the left is the way to the tiny pier. Opposite is a lane to the North Ronaldsay bird observatory, set on the croft of Twingness.

5 Return along the lane and turn left, away from the pier. Look left to see a standing stone over 13ft high. The hole through its upper part is thought to have been used, in conjunction with a stone circle, as a calendar. Carry on to see Holland House, owned by a descendant of the family who bought North Ronaldsay in the 18th century. Standing in front of the house are three cannons salvaged from a ship, *Crown Prince*, that was wrecked in 1744.

ALONG THE WAY

North Ronaldsay has a population of 92. Its narrow roads, almost traffic-free, are a joy to walk. The sheep dyke that surrounds the island is 13 miles long and 5–6ft high. It is occasionally breached during severe weather and the islanders give much of their time to its repair.

The wall keeps the unique North Ronaldsay sheep off pastureland. These hardy animals feed on seaweed and a little thin grass that occasionally grows outside the walls. Close to lambing time the ewes are allowed on to pastures inside the walls for a few weeks and then the ewes and lambs return to the shore.

In summer the island is alive with the calls of breeding birds, many nesting close to the edge of the roads. Look for Arctic terns, redshanks, curlews, skylarks, snipe and cormorants among others. Common and grey seals are numerous and breed around the island.

FACT FILE

Distance 4–9 miles, depending on time of return flight
Time 5–7 hours
Map OS Landranger 5
Start Airport, grid ref 755535
Terrain Generally easy walking except for parts of the beach
Nearest town Kirkwall
Refreshments Small café at the post office

Public transport One boat a week serves the island, weather permitting. Times vary. It docks at the pier for a very short time. Loganair does a good daily cheap flight (except Sundays), which gives you between 5 and 8 hours on the island. For details of times, tel 01856 872494
Stiles None
Suitable for Children, dogs on leads

ORKNEY

NATURAL HISTORY

Visit an island rich in birdlife and archaeological sites.

1 Visit the castle and then walk left (west). At the T junction turn left again. At the next junction take the right fork and continue to pass Noup Farm. Go on up the continuing rough track to the lighthouse.

2 Walk south along the magnificent Old Red Sandstone cliffs. The horizontal rock structure, made of innumerable 'plates' of rock, provides unlimited sites for nesting birds. The smell from the droppings can be overpowering. The nearby waters provide a large amount of food for this huge number of birds. Head south along the spectacular cliffs with the sea to your right, to pass the geos (rocky inlets) and John Harcus Windows, some big caves. Just before you descend The Hammar, the Gentlemen's Cave lies in the sea cliffs far below. Strike inland to climb North Hill to the trig point for a fantastic view towards the island of Rousay.

3 Drop down to join the track walked earlier. Turn right and return to the T junction before the castle.

4 Ignore the right turn and go ahead to follow the reinforced cart track to its end. Go through a metal gate on the right on to the links of Noltland. Look for the many stone walls for drying seaweed. Continue over the short turf, following the fence towards the sandy bay. Turn right and walk along the coast, past shallow depressions where seaweed was burned to produce kelp, once used in glass and soap making and for obtaining iodine.

5 Over the wire fencing on the right, among dunes, is an archaeological dig. Here in the 1970s a prehistoric settlement was excavated. The houses date from about 3000 BC. Carry on to cross a small burn and continue along the links until you reach an Orkney gate (three strands of barbed wire). Once through, turn right and walk along the wide track. To head back to your car, turn right. To return to Pierowall, turn left.

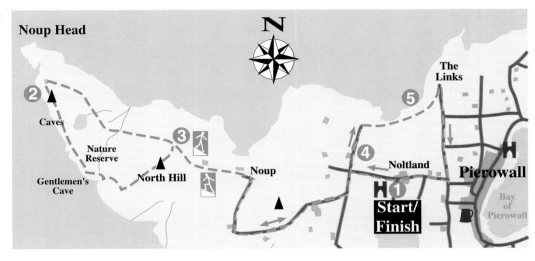

The cliffs at Noup Head

ALONG THE WAY

Lying 24 miles north-west of Kirkwall, Westray is a wonderful island for walking and birdwatching. The RSPB reserve at Noup Head provides a breeding ground for thousands of pairs of guillemots, razorbills, fulmars and kittiwakes.

The Noup Head lighthouse was built in 1898 to warn ships off the North Shoal, which lies off the north-west coast of Orkney. The lighthouse was made automatic in 1964.

Gentlemen's Cave can be reached from the clifftop, but you are advised not to attempt the descent without a local guide. Several Orkney lairds 'retired' to this cave after supporting the 1745 Jacobite Rebellion until their unfortunate allegiance was forgotten. Legend links the cave with Noltland Castle, which was erected in the second half of the 16th Century.

FACT FILE

Distance 10 miles
Time 5 hours
Map OS Landranger 5
Start/parking Close to Noltland Castle. Don't obstruct the entrance to the farm – from where you get the key to visit. Grid ref 429488. Mention to the farmer that you hope to walk over the links, part of his land
Terrain Level walking over the links. Easy walking on Noup Head. Beware dangerous cliffs!
Nearest town Pierowall
Refreshments Pierowall Hotel and Cleaton House Hotel
Public transport The Orkney Islands Shipping Company (OISC) sails to Pierowall twice a week. During summer months OISC operates a three times a day service to Rapness Jetty with a bus link to Pierowall. Loganair flies to Westray daily. There is no public transport from Pierowall to Noltland (½ mile each way)
Stiles None
Suitable for Older children. All dogs on leads

ISLAND HERITAGE

Enjoy a fascinating walk around the island of Rousay and visit an RSPB reserve.

1 From the pier, walk along the road to the T junction. Turn left, where a neat well-cut fuchsia hedge borders the way. Continue past Trumland House on the right, a Jacobean-style mansion. Pass the woodland of the stately home and go through the kissing gate above and to your right.

2 Continue for another 2½ miles. There are glorious views over Eynhallow Sound, with its fierce tidal race. To your right tower the

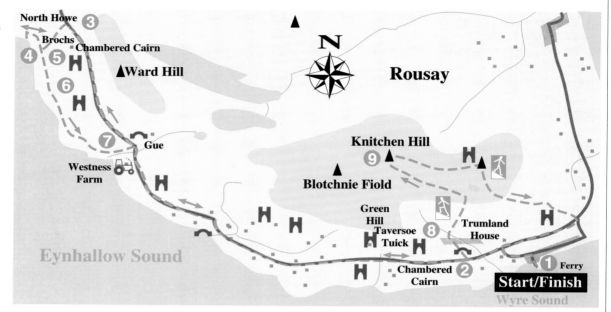

slopes of Blotchnie Fiold and Ward Hill. Pass through the settlement of Gue, a farm and cottages, and walk on for another mile to the signposted layby for the Westness Walk.

3 Follow the signpost on the left for Mid Howe Cairn and Mid Howe Broch to pass the kissing gate. Drop down the steepish slope to a black and white post and continue to another gate and then a second post. Carry on beside the wall on your right. Pass through the next signposted pasture to another gate. Walk right along the shore to a huge, sturdily constructed shed that shields a neolithic chambered cairn from the elements.

4 Continue along the shore to see Mid Howe broch, constructed three or four millennia later than the cairn. Return along the shore past the cairn. Continue on to the ruin of 18th-century Brough Farm, which has gable ends and a cupboard remaining.

5 Pass through a kissing gate and turn right to pass behind the Wirk, once a ceremonial hall, dating from the 13th or 14th century. Cross the stile almost immediately on your right into the churchyard of the ruined former church of Rousay.

6 From the churchyard continue to the next kissing gate, through the ruined Skaill Farm. Carry on around Moa Ness promontory.

7 Continue to the kissing gate just before Westness Farm and walk beside the wall on your right. Go through the next gate to walk along the farm access track. Turn left to walk to the road. Turn right to walk for 2½ miles along the road to the gate on your left. Pass through the gate, signposted Taversoe Tuick cairn. To gain access to the cairn, take the track past it to a gate at the top of its enclosure. Return to the track and continue uphill to a white-topped post, the first of many, to direct you to the reserve. Go on to cross a narrow ford, then an old dyke and a ditch.

8 Follow the posts right and climb through the heather. At the next marker post turn left. Carry on climbing steadily, following the path as it curves right. At the next post, the path is indistinct so find the driest way to the next post (marked 2). Continue left along an old peat track. Cross the peat cuttings, following the posts, and continue climbing. Continue to post 3.

9 Walk east along the ridge, following a line of marker posts which direct you toward a prominent cairn and trig point on Knitchen Hill. Drop down from the cairn to follow the posts over acres of heather and another peat track. Follow the track left to a marker post at the dyke between the moorland and the arable land. Cross the plank bridge, turn left and climb the stile. Cross a pasture to a stile to the road and turn right. Turn left at the signpost for the pier.

A small community would once have lived at Mid Howe Broch

FACT FILE

Distance 10 miles
Time 5–6 hours
Map OS Landranger 6
Start The pier, Rousay, grid ref 436275
Parking At the pier, both at Tingwall on Mainland and Rousay
Terrain Parts of the walk can be rough and wet
Nearest town Kirkwall
Refreshments None on route
Public transport The ferry Eynhallow leaves from Tingwall on the north-east coast of Mainland. The journey across Eynhallow Sound and Wyre Sound takes 20 minutes and there are five or six crossings a day. The pierhead at Rousay has excellent facilities. Tel 01856 75360
Stiles Two
Suitable for Older children

ALONG THE WAY

Rousay lies across Eynhallow Sound from the mainland. It is a hilly island with much heather moorland. This walk follows the Westness Heritage Route and returns through the RSPB Trumland Reserve. Inside Mid Howe cairn, walk round the stalled, chambered cairn, the longest in Orkney, and climb to the slatted platforms above for an exciting view. Look down to where the remains of 25 people were found lying facing inwards on the benches, chambers and floor, in compartments formed by upright slabs.

Mid Howe broch, a fine defensive structure which could house a small community, stands on the rocky shore. On the landward side a strong wall stands between two ditches.

15

HEATHER AND HAUNTINGS

Bounded by rolling dunes and the crashing Atlantic waves, Sandwood Bay is a spectacular stretch of sand in the far north. Its remoteness – the only way in is on foot – means that it remains unspoilt.

1 Leave your car on a grassy parking area on the south side of the road and then set off up the track signed to Sandwood. Go through a gate, then follow the way through an area of sheep grazing to Loch na Gainimh. As you pass along by the loch keep an eye out to the left for a rock with a painted sign indicating the way to Cape Wrath.

2 At the east corner of the lochan, the track reaches a junction. Turn left and it passes down between Loch na Gainimh and a smaller patch of water to your right.

3 As you approach Loch a'Mhuilinn, the track deteriorates into a path. Follow the sandy beach anti-clockwise around the water, then take the path as it rises up over the open moorland. You pass another couple of lochans before you reach the bay.

4 Make your way down over the grass to the dunes. To the right you will see the ruin of a cottage. This is said to be haunted by an old mariner who appears before walkers spending the night in this draughty bothy. Carry on to the mile-long stretch of sand and look south to a spectacular stack in the sea called Am Buachaille (the herdsman).

5 Cross the beach and head over the moorland on the north side of Sandwood Loch. There is no path but follow the lochside and the way is obvious. Head through Strath Shinary to Strathan bothy.

6 Over the Lon Mor from Strathan, an obvious path climbs up out of the glen. It rises through the low heather and grass and skirts round the shores of Loch Mor a'Chraisg.

7 The path is obvious around the loch but becomes a little lost in peat bogs at the far side. However, head towards a small grassy mound and then occasional fence posts keep you on the right track. The path is a little frustrating here as it rises and falls over watery troughs in the peat.

8 A track runs down to the road. When you reach the tarmac, turn right and head back to Blairmore.

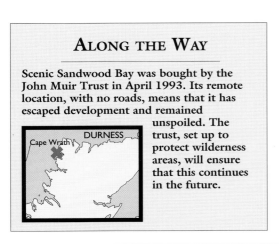

ALONG THE WAY

Scenic Sandwood Bay was bought by the John Muir Trust in April 1993. Its remote location, with no roads, means that it has escaped development and remained unspoiled. The trust, set up to protect wilderness areas, will ensure that this continues in the future.

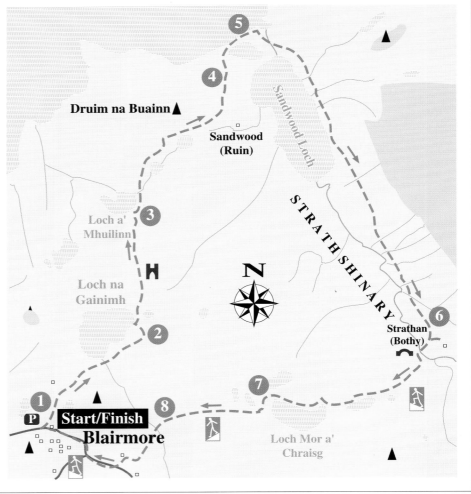

Magnificent Atlantic breakers in Sandwood Bay, with the sea stack of Am Buachaille in the background

FACT FILE

Distance 12 miles
Time 5 hours
Map OS Landranger 9
Start/Parking Blairmore, grid ref 195601
Terrain Track and path over open moorland
Nearest town Ullapool
Refreshments London Store at Achriesgill and Rhiconich Hotel
Public transport None
Stiles None
Suitable for Fit walkers who enjoy a challenge and the remoteness. No dogs

GLORIES OF LEWIS

The drama and beauty of Lewis await you on this fascinating walk from Lionel.

1 From Lionel Old School on the B8013 walk down the road (north). Pass through a gate on the right just before the church hall on your right. Walk ahead, across the machair, a riot of colour provided by pink clover, hay rattle, buttercups, self heal and yellow hawkweed. Climb the stile and pass between the houses of Fivepenny to the road. Turn left.

2 Walk along the road to Eoropie. Look on the right for the sign for St Molua's church, where Episcopalian services are occasionally held. Go inside and enjoy its peace, then walk on to the crossroads where you turn right.

3 Walk along the narrow road towards the coast, passing through a large area of lazybeds. Look right to see the interesting folding of pink Lewisian gneiss, Scotland's most ancient rock. Continue along the curving road to the lighthouse. Sit on a rock and enjoy this dramatic point, where great expanses of ocean stretch away to the north, east and west.

4 Continue past the lighthouse to climb a stile. Carry on with care to walk on the springy turf of the cliffs. Go through the gate in the fence and follow the curving coastline to see the rocky island of Luchruban. It was once said to have been inhabited by pygmies in prehistoric times, but the tiny bones found there are now thought to be of small mammals and birds eaten by a hermit.

5 Continue around the indented coastline, where sea thrift colours the grass and mushrooms grow in profusion. Climb the stile over the fence and go along lower cliffs, where waves crash on the rocky shore.

6 As you continue on the cliffs, look back to see the natural arch in the jutting headland, known as the Eye of the Butt. Go through a gate to walk around the lovely sandy bay of Eoropie.

7 When you reach the south end of the bay climb the low cliffs. Bear left to walk past the radio mast and to the left of the cemetery – placed, like many on Lewis, on a slope close to the sea. Join a tarmacked road and walk along it. Bear left across the machair in the direction of Lionel to pass through a gate. Carry on to the next gate and continue along the fenced grassy track. Pass the township's school. At the police station turn right to rejoin your car.

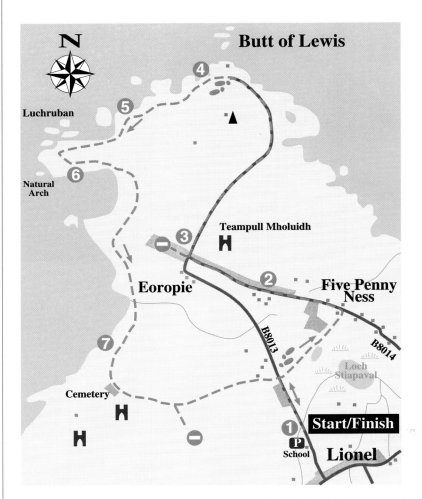

FACT FILE

Distance 6½ miles
Time 3–4 hours
Map OS Landranger 8
Start/parking Lionel Old School, grid ref 525635
Terrain Generally level walking. Care should be taken on cliff tops. Some boggy sections after heavy rain
Nearest town Stornoway
Refreshments Lionel Old School serves teas in summer
Public transport From Stornoway every Friday and Saturday. Leave at 1.15pm, return 7pm. Tel 01851 704327
Stiles Very few, all easy
Suitable for Accompanied children, dogs on leads

The red brick lighthouse on the Butt of Lewis was built in 1862

ALONG THE WAY

As you stand on the Butt of Lewis, the headland that juts out between the Atlantic and the Minch, you can see the dramatic lighthouse. When you hear it mentioned in the weather reports on Radio 4, remember this glorious point.

Outside each house in Eoropie stands an oblong mound of peat. Peat cutting irons, specific to Lewis, are used by crofters to cut the sods. This is done in late spring and they are dried throughout the summer. As you walk through the small settlement, the evocative reek of the fuel hangs in the air.

On your way towards the lighthouse, look for extensive areas of lazybeds on either side of the road. Crofters found it difficult to grow anything in the very shallow wet soils, but lazybeds solved this problem. Strips 6ft wide were covered with soil from ditches dug on either side. This provided both a greater depth of soil and better drainage for potatoes.

TO THE LIGHTHOUSE

While on Harris, set aside a day for a ferry trip to Scalpay. Walk through the delightful island to the lighthouse, Eilean Glas, from where there are superb views to the Shiant Isles and the mountains of Skye.

1 From the ferry, follow the road right and then left as it swings over a bridge. Continue past the school and the community centre. Pass the Scotland Free Church, high on the hill on the left. Carry on past the Church of Scotland.

2 Follow the road as it winds through the island. About 2 miles from the ferry, climb a hill, turn left, and follow the road to a gate that has an arrow and a notice saying 'To the lighthouse'. Go through the next gate and take the narrow stile on the right.

3 Beyond, walk the short narrow valley between two long outcrops of gneiss (laminated rock). Look for the red disc fixed, at shoulder height, to a telegraph pole. These red discs take you over the moorland. The way lies left after the short valley, then goes seawards before heading left again. This change of direction is repeated twice to bring you to a gate in a wall.

4 Pass through the gate and continue towards the next disc. Shortly afterwards the lighthouse comes into view. Walk round the harbour, then over the isthmus of gneiss towards the lighthouse.

5 To return, retrace your outward journey, or you may want to cross the moorland by another route. If so, head from the lighthouse, aiming for a red-topped yellow plastic pole. This leads to another gate in the same wall, to the right of a small loch. Follow the tall, thin yellow posts across the moorland to the side of a small generator and a road. Continue until you reach the gates you passed through earlier.

6 Return along the narrow road to the ferry, enjoying the views of the Clisham range ahead.

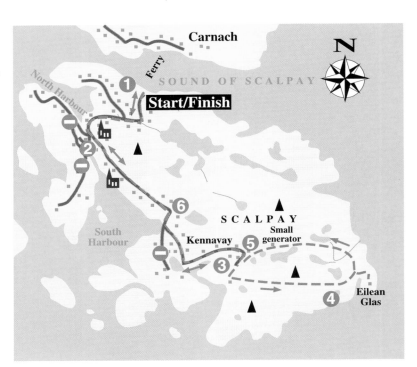

The peaceful island of Scalpay

ALONG THE WAY

The tiny island of Scalpay is only 3 miles long and 1½ miles across, but it is home to a variety of wildlife, and has wonderful walks. In summer, the low heath-clad island supports a wealth of wild flowers and the seashore resounds with the calls of waders and gulls. The sea has always provided a livelihood and the many fishing vessels catch scallops, prawns and lobsters. The indented coastline cuts the land into small peninsulas that can be seen to your right throughout much of the walk. Eilean Glas, constructed in 1788, was one of the first lighthouses built in Scotland. The present tower, on its dramatic promontory, was designed by Robert Stevenson, the grandfather of Robert Louis Stevenson.

FACT FILE

Distance 7 miles
Time 3–4 hours
Map OS Landranger 14
Start Scalpay ferry terminal, grid ref 221971
Parking Space for several cars at the small ferry terminal, Kyles of Scalpay. This lies 5 miles from Tarbert, Harris, on the Scalpay Road
Terrain Easy road walking, with a steepish hill towards the end. The walk over moorland can be wet
Nearest town Tarbert on Harris
Refreshments At the community centre and the small grocery shop
Public transport The Caledonian MacBrayne ferry crossing takes 10 minutes, is inexpensive for foot passengers, and operates 10 to 12 crossings a day
Stiles One, rather narrow
Suitable for Children, dogs on leads

SKYE WALKING

A coastal path leads you into the shadow of the Cuillin mountains and the bay at Camasunary. You can spot the islands of Rhum, Canna and Soay on a clear day.

1 The car park is part way down a steep road to the harbour and as a result the first stretch requires a hard climb back up. But just as you run out of puff, a signpost for Garsbheinn points down a track to the left. This passes a couple of houses and then goes through a gate into a house at the end. Don't go through the gate, take a small path to the right, signed to Loch Coruisk.

2 The path takes you out over grazing land high above the swirling sea. There are excellent views towards the Cuillins ahead, the island of Soay immediately west, Rhum further south and, in the distance between them, Canna. The path falls to cross a burn then continues along the coast. The slope is steep in places with quite a drop below, but it flattens out as it descends to the beach at the end of Glen Scaladal.

3 Cross the burn and then the path climbs up on the far side of the stony shore. Make sure that the path you take runs above the trees as there is a sheep track below which goes nowhere. Back up on the cliffs, proceed with caution and keep young children and dogs in check. The slope becomes steeper before you emerge over a grassy field and the path crosses a stile and runs round to the beach at Camasunary.

4 Walk along the beach which is overshadowed by Bla Bheinn up behind it. At the east end of the beach, a track crosses a bridge then rises up over the hillside. The climb is hard going and a shortcut halfway up takes out one of the loops. The track to Camasunary was built in 1968 by the army. From the top, descend towards Kilmarie, a small cluster of houses.

5 At the road, where there is a small car park, turn right and follow the road back to Elgol. It is a quiet single-track route but keep an eye out for traffic.

Camasunary Bay

ALONG THE WAY

The mountains of the Cuillin are the most challenging and possibly most spectacular in Scotland. Airy ridges and dramatic drops mean you need to have a real head for heights when tackling them and some of the peaks can only be attempted if you have rock climbing and scrambling skills. Perhaps the best known of these is Sgurr Dearg.

FACT FILE

Distance 9 miles
Time 4 hours
Map OS Landranger 32
Start/parking Elgol car park, grid ref 519137
Terrain Path and track along coast steep in places and over open moorland. A head for heights is needed in places
Nearest town Broadford
Refreshments Plenty in Broadford. Small shop in Elgol
Public transport Post bus to Elgol, runs out late morning from Broadford and departs 2.30pm for return
Stiles Two
Suitable for Children and dogs

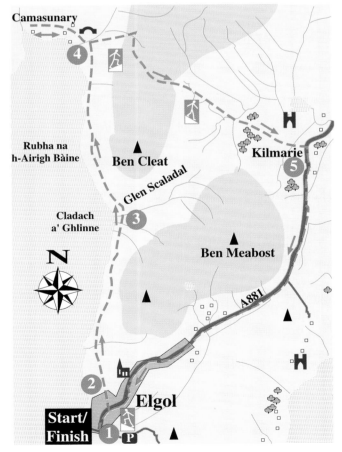

THE GIANT'S ISLAND

Walk around the beautiful green island of Berneray in the Sound of Harris, visiting a knoll of skulls, a giant's memorial and Viking chairstones.

1 Leave the jetty and follow the road right, continuing past the little harbour of Poll an Oir. Carry on to pass the jetty at Loch a Bhasigh, where the passenger ferry to Harris calls on request. The jetty and harbour buildings were erected in 1988 and are owned by the island's Council. Go on round Bays Loch. Notice the shop on the left because this is where you turn off the road later for your walk along the sands. Carry on towards the school, which you reach by taking the right fork, where the road divides.

2 Just before the school, at Ruisgarry, look right to see several blackhouses. These were occupied until the late 1970s, when the people were rehoused. Much of the old furniture can still be seen but the weather will soon destroy this fascinating reminder of the past. Walk on round the headland towards the youth hostel, where several blackhouses have been carefully restored to accommodate 14 visitors. Continue along the road to view the ruins of a church on a hill to your left. This was built by the 19th-century engineer Thomas Telford and was used by the people of Berneray and the nearby island of Pabbay.

3 Return along the coast road, past the shop noted earlier, and take a narrow road, signposted to Brusda, on the right. The road climbs gently through green fields and then drops steadily. Where it swings sharply left, continue ahead along a reinforced track, keeping to the right of a crofthouse. Beyond a gate the track leads to another gate which you pass through. Beyond, a wide grassy track winds over the magnificent machair. Go through a gate into the dunes and follow the way through a wall of sand and marram 20–30ft high, to walk down on to the splendid west beach.

4 Turn left to walk on the shell sand. Over the water you can see the island of Pabbay. Walk along the sand for 2½ miles. The next green island you see is Boreray. Leave the beach just where the low cliffs begin, to pick up one of several grassy tracks winding through the sand dunes and then over the machair. The track passes below the ruins of a herdsman's hut on the Knoll of Skulls. Climb the small hill and look north over a vast stretch of machair.

5 Now walk on, heading east towards a tall man-made cairn, which is surrounded by a small wall and odd stones. It commemorates a giant, Angus MacAskill. Carry on along the edge of the Sound, heading towards a walled burial ground. Continue along the low headland until the sea loch, Loch Borve, comes into view. As you near the loch, join a grassy track that runs beside it. Cross a small stone bridge over a tributary stream and then press ahead across the machair to join a reinforced track that leads to the community centre.

6 Walk in front of the centre and pass through a gate on its right. Strike ahead, bearing slightly left, towards a number of boulders. Look for two that are shaped like seats. These chairstones are believed to date from Viking times and were used during the settling of disputes. Return to the centre and follow the track left to walk through Borve, a village built in 1900. At the T junction turn right to return to the ferry.

FACT FILE

Distance 10 miles
Time 5 hours
Map OS Landranger 18
Start Jetty at Berneray's southernmost tip, grid ref 915799
Parking Both jetties
Terrain Easy walking all the way. Can be wet underfoot. Sands exposed to west winds
Nearest towns Lochmaddy, North Uist
Refreshments The Lobster Pot tea room opens Monday–Saturday. The community centre in Borve is open July–August, Tuesday–Saturday
Public transport The crossing from Otternish (called Newton Ferry by local people) to Berneray takes 10 minutes. Tel 018767 230
Stiles None
Suitable for All ages

ALONG THE WAY

The machair is a fertile strip that lies behind the extensive dune system. Rye, oats and potatoes are grown in rotation in large strips. Growing among the cereals are great banks of corn marigolds and red poppies.

The tall man-made cairn was erected in 1991 to commemorate Angus MacAskill, who lived almost 130 years ago. Angus, a giant 7ft 9in tall, was born in a croft on the site of the cairn. He left Berneray when he was six, emigrating with his family to Nova Scotia. He was reputed to be the strongest man in the world.

The memorial to the giant Angus MacAskill at point 5

FAIRIES IN THE WOODS

Follow a woodland glen, look out over the Moray Firth and visit a lighthouse, all on the Black Isle.

1 From the car park, join the path beside the burn and turn upstream, passing under the red sandstone road bridge. Join a tarmac driveway for 40yds before the path forks off to the right again. Small ponds in this area were once used for soaking flax to soften the fibres before it was made into linen. From the millpond, ice used to be cut to preserve salmon caught at nearby fishing stations. Cross the stream and millpond by wooden footbridges. Pass two waterfalls and cross more bridges.

2 Emerge on to the A832 and turn left. Although this is a main road without a footpath, you only follow it for ⅓ mile and traffic is not heavy.

3 Turn left by the 'phone box at the sign to Raddery and after 150yds cross a stone bridge and turn left again at the sign for Mid-Craiglands. Before the first bend, look back over the ridges and valleys that run from south-west to north-east along the length of the Black Isle. Beyond, you can see Ben Wyvis.

4 As you begin to descend towards the Moray Firth, pause to take in the extensive views. Look east down the firth as far as Burghead, 28 miles away. Swinging to the right, you see the cranes of Ardersier oil platform construction yard, then Fort George with Chanonry Ness below you, and up the Inverness Firth to the Kessock Bridge and Inverness. With luck, you may see right along the Great Glen to Ben Nevis, 65 miles away. Continue the descent into Fortrose.

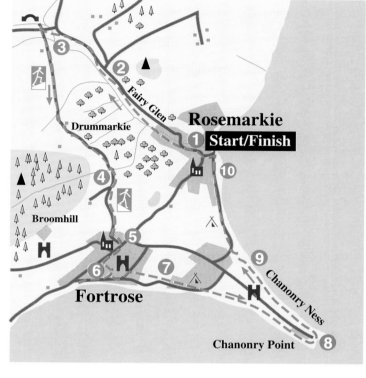

5 Turn right into the main street by the church with the spire. Turn left at the Royal Hotel and go round Cathedral Square to the opposite corner. Turn left to walk along Academy Street.

6 A short detour down St Andrew's Walk takes you to the tiny harbour, built by Thomas Telford. The fishing fleet has now given way to yachts. Return and continue along Academy Street, turning left into Deans Road with school buildings on your right. Take the first right with playing fields on your left. Follow a wide grassy track almost to the shore.

7 Continue ahead on a minor road which takes you through Fortrose Caravan Park. At the end a sign indicates the footpath along the western edge of Chanonry Ness.

8 Chanonry Point, with its lighthouse at the extreme tip, is one of the best spots from which to watch for the Moray Firth's resident group of bottlenose dolphins. They are most likely to be seen on the flood tide. Look at the nearby icehouses before picking up the path along the eastern side of the ness and making for Rosemarkie.

9 Where the path ends by the golf clubhouse, join the seafront road which passes through another caravan site to Rosemarkie.

10 MacFarquhar's Kitchen is a convenient place to stop for refreshment. Continue to the very end of the seafront, turning inland. Join the main street and go ahead towards the car park – but stop on the way to look up to the sandy cliff on the right where fulmar petrels nest.

FACT FILE

Distance 6½ miles
Time 3½ hours
Map OS Landranger 27
Start/parking Free car park for Fairy Glen by A832 on northern edge of Rosemarkie, grid ref 736578
Terrain Wooded riverside glen, country lanes, small towns, coastal spit
Nearest town Rosemarkie
Refreshments In Fortrose and Rosemarkie

Public transport Highland bus service 26 Inverness to Rosemarkie throughout the day Monday to Saturday
Stiles None
Suitable for Children and dogs

ALONG THE WAY

The Fairy Glen is a valuable wildlife habitat, maintained by the RSPB. There is an information board in the car park explaining what you might see. The glen is always damp, so care is needed on a few steps of polished rock.

Fortrose cathedral was built early in the 13th century for the diocese of Ross. By the 1620s it was in poor repair and it fell out of use by the end of the century. The ruins are open at all times.

Glaciers once carried a medley of rocks towards the sea, depositing them to form features such as Chanonry Ness. Rosemarkie is famous for the sculptured stones of Pictish origin at Groam House Museum.

The harbour at Fortrose, formerly a fishing port

FOREST AND FIRTHS

Free your spirit on this varied route which includes imposing views over two firths and a delightful woodland path.

1 Cross the A9 between two wooden gates, one on each side of the road. Follow the path ahead from the northern car park for 100yds, through a wooden kissing gate, and turn right along the hillside. Take in the view of the Beauly Firth, the Kessock Bridge and part of the Moray Firth.

2 Immediately before the next gate, turn left uphill at a blue-banded marker post, climbing wooden steps. Roe or Sika deer may be seen in the forest. At the forest road, turn left.

3 Turn left at the cross tracks, and pass Ordhill forest walks car park 20yds before reaching a road.

4 Turn right on to the road, following it through the forest.

5 For the shorter route, turn right at the sign for Kilmuir and follow the road to point 11. For the longer route, the road now passes between the large fields of a tree nursery.

6 Ignore the turning to the buildings at Pitlundie and keep on to the end of the tarmac road at grid ref 676513.

7 Turn right on to a gravel road for 50yds.

8 At a gateway in the road where there is a sign 'Taindore House', turn right on to a path, initially with a fence on the left. Pass through birch wood and out on to heathland to a viewpoint. To the north you see the depression in which lies Munlochy Bay, a popular spot for watching ducks and waders. Continue on the path, crossing a grassy track into birch wood. The path becomes indistinct over several rocky vantage points, but is clear in the vegetation between them. Where the route divides into two equally well-trodden paths, take the left, passing a viewpoint before descending. Continue through larch, then Scots pine, to see the end of Loch Lundin on the right.

9 Turn away from the loch and continue on the path, ignoring the wheel ruts made by forestry machinery. As the path descends, it winds back towards the north-east and emerges on to a minor road.

10 Turn left and follow the road to the shore by Kilmuir old cemetery and church ruins.

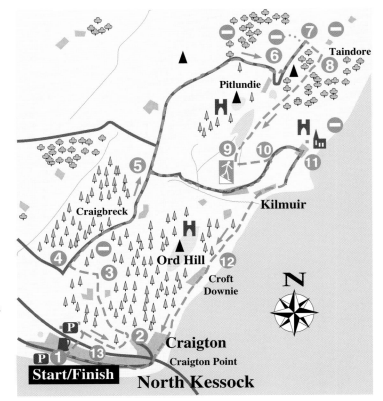

11 Turn right along the attractive village waterfront, taking to the beach after the last house. Remember that the next 500yds are covered at high water, and rock scrambling to get past is not advisable.

12 Just before an old iron shed on the beach, the path enters a wood and after 100yds merges with a track. After 20yds, avoid a drive marked 'private' by forking right on to an old tarmac road. About 200yds further on, turn left down a short zigzag path to another tarmac road and turn right. Follow this under Kessock Bridge to North Kessock.

13 Here you can enjoy refreshment while looking out over the former Kessock ferry crossing and scanning the water for leaping dolphins. Steps take you up to the car park.

Distance 5½ or 7½ miles
Time 2½ or 3½ hours
Map OS Landranger 26
Start/parking Tourist Information Centre at North Kessock, beside A9,1 mile north of Kessock Bridge, grid ref 655480
Terrain Forest tracks, minor roads, woodland paths, foreshore
Nearest town Inverness
Refreshments Various in North Kessock
Public transport Hourly bus service 26A from Inverness to North Kessock
Stiles None
Suitable for Older children and dogs

ALONG THE WAY

Parts of this wonderful walk are a haven for wildlife. Near the beginning quiet progress may be rewarded by the sight of deer, while patience near the end may result in the sight of dolphins. There is a car park on each side of the A9 which has a central barrier, so which side you park depends on the direction in which you are driving. Make sure you time your walk to avoid the beach section between points 11 and 12 during the last two hours before high water. There is no convenient alternative to walking along the top of the pebble and rock beach, which is covered by the highest tides.

Enjoy this view of Beauly Firth near the start of the walk

PARADISE ISLAND

Wander the island of Ulva, with its stunning scenery and fascinating history.

1 Leave the tearoom to walk left (south) along the reinforced track to a six-armed signpost. Bear left for the basalt rocks and go on beside the glorious deciduous woodland of Ulva House. This was built in the 1950s on the site of a large, early 19th-century house, which was destroyed by fire. Ignore the turning on the left and continue towards Bracadale Farm. Just before the outbuildings, follow the signpost to walk left along a walled track and out on to open pasture towards the sea. Go through the next gate to stand on a small headland with a grand view across the sea. Here you can see the basalt columns formed when a volcano near Ben More poured out molten lava. Glacial action resulted in the columns of lava cooling quickly and crystallising. Inland, on the site of an old fort, Dun Bhioramuill, stands the burial ground of the Clark family. The huge marble monuments lie inside a high gateless wall. Sir Francis Clark bought Ulva in 1835 and cared well for the island's community, which thrived on the kelp industry.

2 Follow the path past lines of lazybeds, where potatoes were grown in the last two centuries. Away to the right of the path, up a slope, tucked into the base of a high basalt stranded cliff, is Livingston's Cave. Here, 200 years ago, the father and grandfather of the missionary and explorer lived while waiting for a house to be built. Descend to a large grassy area, cross a ditch and climb a slope to see a similar house to the one in which Livingston's family lived.

3 Follow the path, which now turns inland and climbs steadily through birch woodland, to join a track that swings left. Go straight on with magnificent views out to sea, then descend to the ruined village of Ormaig. In the early 19th century 600 people lived in 16 villages. By 1851 the population had been reduced to 150, and today only 25 people live on Ulva. Go on to the head of a small muddy tidal inlet to see an old cruck mill.

4 Walk on along the track to the ruined village of Cragaig, then continue to Kilvekewan. Drop down the slopes, seaward, to the graveyard. Here several MacQuaries are buried. Lachlan MacQuarie was the most famous of the clan. He entertained Dr Johnson and James Boswell on Ulva in 1773.

5 Return along the track to where you joined it above the birch wood. From here there is a good view of Eas Fors waterfall, on Mull, plummeting magnificently over the cliff. Go on along the well-signposted track to the ferry, perhaps with just enough time for refreshments before taking the last ferry to Mull.

FACT FILE

Distance 10 miles
Time 5–6 hours
Maps OS Landranger 48, OS Pathfinder 32 & 33. Map in visitor's guide
Start The pier on Ulva, grid ref 444395
Parking At Ulva Ferry on Mull
Terrain Generally easy walking unless you leave the path
Nearest town Tobermory on Mull
Refreshments The Boathouse Tearoom and Visitor Centre, Ulva
Public transport Foot passengers on ferry to Ulva; bikes can be taken. No public transport to Ulva Ferry. Ferry Sailings from Ulva Ferry to Ulva Monday–Friday 0900–1700 on the hour, Sundays June 1 to Sept 15 only (on the hour). Ferry closed all day Saturday. October 15 to April 15 – ferry by arrangement. Tel 016885 264 or 226
Stiles None
Suitable for Older children. All dogs on leads – no dogs April and May (lambing time)

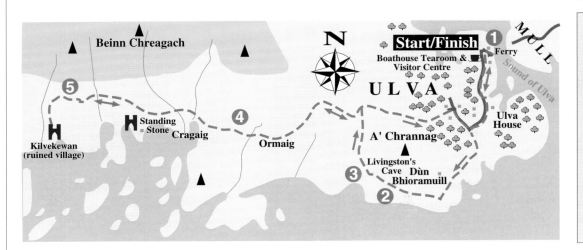

ALONG THE WAY

Before setting off on your walk around Ulva call at the interpretive museum above the Boathouse Tearoom which serves excellent homemade food and even oysters and a glass of wine. Five walks, of varying length, are sensitively signposted or waymarked with white painted stones or plain wooden posts. Visitors are invited to follow these or blaze their own trails.

ON THE ROCKS

Walk over a magnificent col on the Isle of Arran and down to the north shore.

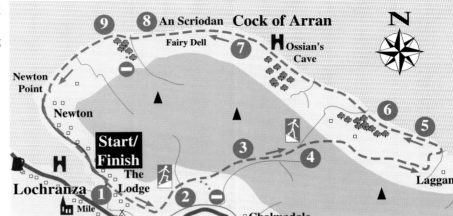

1 From the parking area on the left, just beyond the Lodge, walk back along the road to the sharp bend and then head along the continuing cart track, signposted to Laggan. After ½ mile take the grassy left branch where the cart track continues ahead to several cottages.

2 Cross the Eadaraidh burn on a footbridge with several planks missing, and then climb the path, looking for deer on the slopes and the outline of the Sleeping Warrior to the right.

3 Near the top of the col pick your way across a wide boggy area. Look right to see piles of slate waste. Slate is one of the oldest rocks on the island (600 million years) and was quarried in the 18th century by workmen who had to walk the hill every morning. From the ridge the view is glorious.

4 The dry, reinforced grassy track descends steadily. Ignore the narrow left turn and drop straight down the steep hillside to the ruins of Cock Farm. Continue until you see another ruined crofthouse below to your left. Just before this, the wide, grassy track swings left and drops steadily downhill to the shore beside Laggan Cottage.

5 Turn left and begin the glorious walk along the raised beach, passing a large area of pale grey sandstone. As you approach a small alder and birch wood, keep to the shore path until you reach the ruins of a small building. Below lies the tiny harbour of Laggan, which was just big enough for the thriving community that once lived here.

6 Carry on along the shore to see two fenced pools on your right. These are shafts from which coal was mined. Carry on along the shore to pass through a gap in an old stone wall. Beyond, to your left, lies Ossian's Cave.

7 Pass a huge sandstone boulder. This is the Cock of Arran, once a landmark for returning fishermen. Continue to pass through the huge rock fall known as An Scriodan. The path runs high above the sea and leads down to the shore beyond. Here look for long sills of hard rock stretching across the beach.

8 Walk on past the cottage at Fairy Dell, which is backed by a glorious pocket of woodland. Go on along the path below the shallow cliffs. At the first stream, turn right to walk to the shore. Here look for Hutton's Unconformity (see Along The Way).

9 From here it is a pleasant stroll to Newton Point. Walk on beside the sea loch, with a grand view of ruined Lochranza Castle, rebuilt in the 16th century. Carry on to rejoin your car.

FACT FILE

Distance 9 miles
Time 5 hours
Map OS Landranger 69
Start/parking South Newton, grid ref 938506
Terrain Steady climb over generally easy path and long easy descent to the shore. The walk along the shore involves some scrambling and boulder-hopping through wet areas
Nearest town Brodick
Refreshments At camp site before milestone 44 on the A841. Jetty café, north-west end of Lochranza
Public transport Caledonian MacBrayne ferry from Ardrossan to Brodick. Tel 01475 650000. Western Scottish Bus, no 324, from Brodick pier, alight at Lochranza Field Centre. Infrequent in winter. Tel 01770 30200
Stiles None
Suitable for Children and dogs

ALONG THE WAY

Dr James Hutton went to Arran on a field trip in 1787 and discovered the island's remarkable variety of rocks. On this walk you can see his most important discovery, known as Hutton's Unconformity. This is a rock formation where red sandstone laid down 400 million years ago tilts towards the sea, overlying schist thought to be about 200 million years older.
Cock Farm is the ancestral home of Daniel Macmillan, the book publisher, born there in 1813.

ROCKY ISLAND

Enjoy a linear walk from the scattered village of Kildonan to see some of the highlights of the Isle of Arran.

1 Walk west along a track beyond the store at Kildonan. Make your way along the path that in some places follows the shore and in others goes over a grassy raised beach. Just beyond the last cottage a waterfall tumbles noisily over a cliff. Go on past another waterfall to a small bay between dykes, where seals bask. Pass two more falls. After a mile the path becomes more rocky and then ceases. Pick your way through the boulders for the last ½ mile before the cave.

2 If the tide is not full, you can walk round the last boulders and into the cave. Otherwise climb round on the conveniently stepped black rocks. Keep just above the shallow water rather than climbing higher over the yellow lichened rocks. The scramble isn't difficult and children should enjoy it.

3 Return by the same route. Continue through Kildonan and take the cart track on the right, leading towards the castle. Pass behind the first cottage on the right and then walk straight ahead when the tarmac ceases. The ruin lies to the left, on a cliff overlooking the sandy beach.

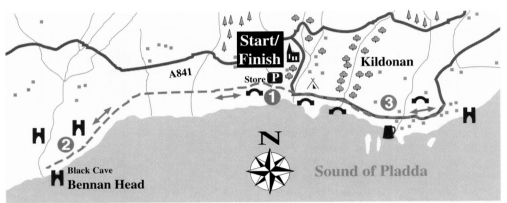

ALONG THE WAY

This pleasant walk is one for all the family. It has singing seals, a multitude of wild flowers, dramatic waterfalls and a huge cave which just might have to be approached by a ledge above the lapping waves. An added option is a visit to Kildonan Castle.

Kildonan, where the walks to the cave and the castle start, is named after St Donan, who went to Arran with St Columba to convert the people to Christianity. It is a scattered village with two hotels and stretches of sand. Black Cave is at the point, Bennan Head; it's cut out of the black smooth rock and has an exit at the back.

The rocky coastline was the scene of innumerable shipwrecks, the subject of many tales. Rocky reefs continue from the shore towards Pladda and its lighthouse. Beyond stands Ailsa Craig. The ruined Kildonan Castle is picturesquely covered with lichen, ivy and sea campion. This medieval keep was first given to John, the bastard son of Robert III, in 1406. It has window openings and arches intact – just enough to set the imagination working.

The rugged splendour of Bennan Head, seen from Kildonan

FACT FILE

Distance 6½ miles
Time 3 hours
Map OS Landranger 69
Start Kildonan village, grid ref 018212
Parking Near the village store
Terrain Shore becomes boulder-strewn just before the cave

Nearest town Brodick
Refreshments Hotels in village, cafés and hotels in Brodick
Public transport Caledonian MacBrayne roll on-roll off ferry from Ardrossan to Brodick, tel 01475 650000. Western Scottish Buses Ltd, tel 01770 302000
Stiles None
Suitable for Children

ISLAND TREASURES

This glorious walk from Kintra farmhouse on the island of Islay features a standing stone, three deserted townships, a magnificent stack, a deep spectacular chasm, two waterfalls, otters, seals and choughs.

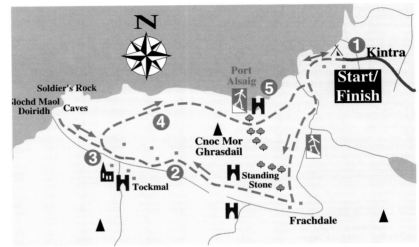

1 With your back to the restaurant, follow the track to the left that winds above the shore. Pass through the gate with a notice saying 'No dogs beyond'. Follow the good track as it moves steadily out into moorland and then leads you towards the ruined crofthouse of Frachdale. Just before the ruin, take the track to the right. As you approach the gate look right to see a tall standing stone. Beyond the gate stroll the sometimes indistinct track as it moves ahead through the heather. Aim for the ruined township of Ghrasdail. Look for the kiln, set into the slope on your right, before you reach the roofless dwellings.

2 Descend steadily left, passing remnants of old walls. Cross a narrow stream to visit Tockmal, where just before the ruined houses stands a cup-marked rock. See if you can find another. Step across a tributary stream to see traces of the chapel and graveyard. Return across the main stream for a drier way and head towards the sea.

3 Before entering the deepening gully through which the stream flows, recross it to go on past an elegant waterfall. Go with care over the natural arch for a good view of the stack, the deep pool and the caves. Look here for choughs. Return along the stream, cross it once more and then head on, east along the coast, keeping high above the shore. Follow helpful sheep tracks as you pick your way over the wild pathless moorland.

4 Continue for a little more than a mile and then begin to descend, choosing the easiest way. There is no footpath. As you near the quartzite cliffs at Port Askaig, find your way through the natural birch woodland; again go the same way as the sheep.

5 Continue around two sandy bays edged with conical grassy peaks to a good farm track. Soon after joining it, head left towards the cliff edge and walk on to see a pretty waterfall on the Abhainn Glas. Rejoin the track and cross the burn on convenient stones or a footbridge upstream. Join your outward track and turn left to return to Kintra.

FACT FILE

Distance 5 miles
Time 3–4 hours
Map OS Landranger 60
Start Kintra, grid ref 321484
Parking Park tidily to the right of the Old Granary Restaurant at Kintra farm
Terrain Good walking on tracks and paths. Can be wet and the going can be rough through the glen. Care is required when descending from the high moorland and through the birch woodland
Nearest towns Bowmore and Port Ellen
Refreshments Old Granary Bar

Restaurant at Kintra
Public transport Car ferry from Kennacraig (West Loch Tarbert) to Port Ellen or Port Askaig. Tel 01880 730253. Bus service 452 Port Askaig to Bowmore; 451 Port Ellen to Bowmore, using Islay Coaches. Tel 0141 226 4826
Stiles None
Suitable for Children, no dogs

ALONG THE WAY

Kintra stands beside 7 miles of sand where bays and dunes are so numerous that there seems to be one each for everyone. Explore the ruined townships of Ghrasdail and Tockmal to find a drying kiln, cup-marked rocks, a chapel and a graveyard. Go carefully as you visit the Soldier's Rock, a fine stack with glistening veins of quartz. Cross a natural arch with the surging Atlantic below. Look into the immensely deep Slochd Maol Doiridh, which is edged by a cave with three entrances. Sit on grassy flats on top of the magnificent cliffs and watch the choughs perform acrobatics in the air currents. Return over the high moorland and then down through the natural birch woodland of an SSSI.

The Soldier's Rock

EVER GREEN

Walk in open forest near Carradale with a detour beside a deep sea loch.

1 Before setting off, take a look at the display board at the picnic place. There is a description of the walk and a large-scale map of the route, together with any adjustments to the route which may have to be made for forestry reasons. From the car park, take the main forestry track which is at right angles to the public road, walking round the metal gate. It is easy walking above and parallel with the road, in open forest at first, giving views across the valley to heather-clad hills, forest and farms.

2 After 2¼ miles, a path branches off right to the Network Centre, a disused sawmill which has been undergoing conversion to an information centre for the area. There is a

small car park and the walk can easily be joined or left using the short path linking the centre to the forest track. Continue along the level forest track, from which there are occasional views down Carradale Bay to Kilbrannan Sound. Picnic tables have thoughtfully been provided along this section.

3 When the track is at its nearest point to Carradale, another track branches off to the right, giving access to the village. This is a suitable start and finish point if you arrive at Carradale by bus. Continue ahead, descending and coming nearer to the shore.

4 After ¾ mile, look out for a handrail and a marker post on the right. Follow the well-made path beside the handrail and descend among trees to the shore.

5 Turn left along the shore, which is composed of rounded pebbles and boulders of metamorphic rock showing fascinating folds of the strata. Behind you, Carradale harbour comes into sight and across Kilbrannan Sound you can see Arran. Follow the shore for about 500yds, numerous marker posts confirming that you have not missed a turn. The pebbles may be covered at high water on spring tides, but there is a trodden path winding through the trees beside the beach.

6 A conspicuous handrail marks the beginning of the easy climb on a well-constructed zigzag path to regain a forest track where you turn right.

7 Follow the track until you see the remains of some buildings on the right. There is an excellent view past the northern tip of Arran to the Cowal peninsula. A small track leads off to the right, but keep to the main track as it swings left, over the ridge, and down towards Glen Carradale and the car park.

8 As the main track bends right, take an old track straight ahead: it leads directly to the car park. If you miss the turn, it doesn't matter as the main track also takes you to the finish.

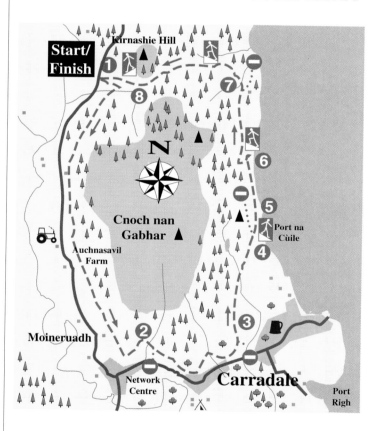

Near the start of the walk, views extend across Glen Carradale to the hills of Kintyre

ALONG THE WAY

Covering forest and sea loch, this route is full of amazing sights. Relish the beauty of the Sitka spruces that never completely enclose you and prepare to gasp at the sight of salmon leaping, seals and just possibly a basking shark in Kilbrannan Sound.

This is one of many forest walks laid out by the Forestry Commission in Knapdale and Kintyre. Each has its own appeal and all are excellently prepared and waymarked. This shore walk is marked by blue footprint symbols on green posts. Carradale, the masts of whose fishing fleet you may see from the shore section of the walk, was the home port of *Antares*, the trawler which was so tragically towed under by a submarine in the Firth of Clyde. A memorial plaque to the four young fishermen who lost their lives can be seen on the harbour wall.

FACT FILE

Distance 6½ miles
Time 2½ hours
Maps OS Landranger 62 & 68
Start/parking Forestry Commission picnic place by B842, 2 miles south of Grogport, grid ref 794413
Terrain Forest roads, pebble shore, well-made paths
Nearest town Campbeltown
Refreshments Pubs, café and restaurant in Carradale
Public transport Several buses daily from Tarbert and Campbeltown to Carradale
Stiles None
Suitable for Children and dogs

HIDDEN TREASURE

A short but exciting stroll to a quiet island that keeps a beautiful secret.

1 Leave the roadside and walk out on to the Doirlinn. The shingle surface gives easy walking. The causeway is about ¾ mile long and bends to the right part way across.

2 At the far side turn right along the stony beach and head for the base of the cliffs ahead. Continue along the now narrow beach, boulder hopping below the steep cliffs. There are several caves, but the entrance leading to the painting is clearly signed. The cave is only a few yards deep so a torch is not needed. The painting is on the left-hand side and, lit by a shaft of light, is most striking. Painting directly on to the rock, MacKinnon used the natural cracks and irregularities on the rock's surface to give a three dimensional appearance.

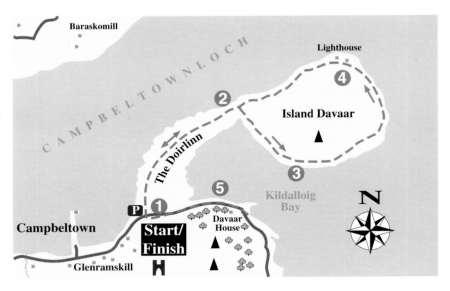

3 If you have time, head up the grassy slopes to the trig point at the island's summit. There are fine views across the loch. Otherwise, from the cave go straight on along the beach, which can be bouldery. When the cliffs peter out, a small path leads up to the lighthouse.

4 From the lighthouse a track takes you past a small jetty and then a path leads back to the Doirlinn. Retrace your route across here to the mainland.

5 For an impressive view of the island, follow the quiet single track road left from the car park. Just beyond Davaar House are some sandy beaches followed by a pebbled one. Retrace your steps to the start.

FACT FILE

Distance 4½ miles
Time 2½ hours
Map OS Landranger 68
Start/parking Car park at grid ref 721205
Terrain Shingle and stony beaches, bouldery in places
Nearest town Campbeltown
Refreshments None on walk
Public transport None to walk. Coach to Campbeltown from Glasgow
Stiles None
Suitable for Older children. Dogs on leads

NB There is plenty of time for this walk between high tides. Check with the tourist information centre on the pier at Campbeltown for tide timetable.

ALONG THE WAY

Guarding the entrance to Campbeltown Loch is the small, uninhabited island of Davaar.

Hidden in a small cave at the base of sheer cliffs is a wonderful painting depicting the crucifixion of Christ. This work of art dates back to 1887 when the local artist, Alexander MacKinnon, worked in secret. The painting was later discovered and in 1934 MacKinnon, aged 80, returned to retouch his work.

A shingle causeway, called the Doirlinn, is exposed at low tide giving access to the island and its treasure.

The impressive island of Davaar

CIRCLE IN THE SAND

Search out the sand among the stones on a trek along the Angus coastline.

1 On the northern edge of the parking area, a track strikes north by a wooden 'Private road - no unauthorised vehicles' sign. Follow this along in front of a row of cottages and it terminates when it reaches a small stream. Cross it to follow the coastal path stretching out ahead along the top of the marram-covered sand dunes. The way is sandwiched between the beach to the right and a wire and post fence, beyond which the main Dundee to Aberdeen railway line runs across open fields.

2 The path and railway converge two-thirds of a mile from the start and run together for a short way – there's a burn to be crossed but a makeshift footbridge is provided next to the track. In places the dunes have been eroded and it is necessary to drop down briefly to the beach .

3 The coastal path and railway part company and after the track turns inland the path meets a line of concrete blocks. These wartime remnants were placed along the top of the beach to prevent army tanks making it ashore in the event of a German landing. The path skirts between the concrete blocks and fence, emerging on to a wide grassy shoulder.

4 Follow the bank beyond a concrete culvert conveying a burn out to sea, then drop down on to the wide sweep of sand that curves north towards Arbroath.

5 The beach is sliced in two by the mouth of the Elliot Water. When you reach the stream, turn left and follow it inland a short distance to a bridge carrying it under the railway. Don't venture on to the railway track, but turn left before the line and follow a path running adjacent to the line. A short way along this, pause by a lagoon on the left where wildfowl and small seabirds congregate on the still water.

6 The path reaches a level crossing. Carry straight ahead on a narrow tarmac roadway running alongside the railway and when this ends, a wide sandy path leads back up on to dunes. Drop down on to the beach and follow it back to Carnoustie.

Elliot

Golf Course

N

Start/ Finish

East Haven

Harbour

The Brithers

ALONG THE WAY

The Angus coast is one of contrasts; high cliffs and craggy, rocky outcrops dominate but every so often the rough edge has been smoothed away by the sea to provide a golden strip of sand.

East Haven, just up the coast from Carnoustie, boasts a sheltered natural harbour where a half-moon of glistening sand nestles between the surrounding rock. Small sailing boats are pulled up on the foreshore and seabirds circle in search of a tasty morsel or two washed in by the North Sea. This is the starting point for a coastal trek north-east towards Arbroath, where a much longer stretch of sand awaits the walker.

FACT FILE

Distance 6 miles
Time 3 hours
Map OS Landranger 54
Start/parking East Haven, near Carnoustie, grid ref 593363. Low bridge under railway line leads to parking area, picnic tables and public toilets
Terrain Coastal path and beach
Nearest town Carnoustie
Refreshments Choice of pubs and cafés in Carnoustie
Public transport Strathtay Scottish bus service No 73 from Dundee via Carnoustie to East Haven
Stiles None
Suitable for All

TAYSIDE

Forfar

Arbroath

Dundee

Perth

St Andrews

Auchterarder

Falkland **FIFE**

Glenrothes

Pittenweem

Cowdenbeath

Buckhaven

Kirkcaldy

North Berwick

The coastal path along the dunes

ON THE BEACH

A pleasant coastal walk along part of the Fife coast path from St Andrews to Crail, with views south over the Forth estuary.

1 On the grassy bank above the beach, a path heads south, rises up towards a caravan park and then follows the cliff-tops away from St Andrews along Kinkell Braes. A short way on a set of steps offers a detour down to the beach and a giant rock. Coastal erosion means that there is slight slippage past the caravan park. If the path disappears at any point you may have to clamber through the caravan park to get back on route.

2 After about 1 mile of flat walking, the path descends to a beach, crossing a fence at a wooden stile. There is a waymarker just beyond this and the path winds through the grass at the top of the sand and stone shoreline. The way skirts round Kinkell Ness to the Rock and Spindle, a large column of rock, part of which is patterned like the spokes of a bicycle wheel. Walk along the beach to a fence and stile.

3 Cross the stile and a narrow path rises up from the foreshore for a short way – take care, as it is quite tricky in one spot. Once over this hurdle, however, you are back on another stretch of beach before the path heads through the grass. It is quite narrow and overgrown in places. Reach a wooden sign which warns that the path may be covered by the tide and follow the foreshore for a very short distance to another overgrown section of path which is signed 'Coastal Walk'. Watch out for the odd nettle, thistle and prickly bramble in the undergrowth.

4 The path rises away from the beach and climbs to a small stone pillar at the corner of a field. It continues along the edge of the field and through open countryside and a grassy field to a dilapidated shed.

5 A signpost gives the distance to Crail as 7 miles and warns that the Kenly burn can only be crossed at low tide. If the tide is out, continue along the coast and take care when crossing the water as the rocks are slippery. If it is in, head inland up the track towards Boarhills. Continue through the village on to the main street.

6 Follow the main street round to a right-hand bend in the road. A track to the left will take you back down to the foreshore.

7 Once over the burn the path runs above the shoreline. A grassy stretch skirts round to Airbow Point. Follow the foreshore to the car park at Cambo Sands.

8 Walk along the beach and rejoin the coastal path at the far end. It runs through a grassy patch round to Cambo Ness where it disappears into the trees for a short time, crossing on a good footbridge.

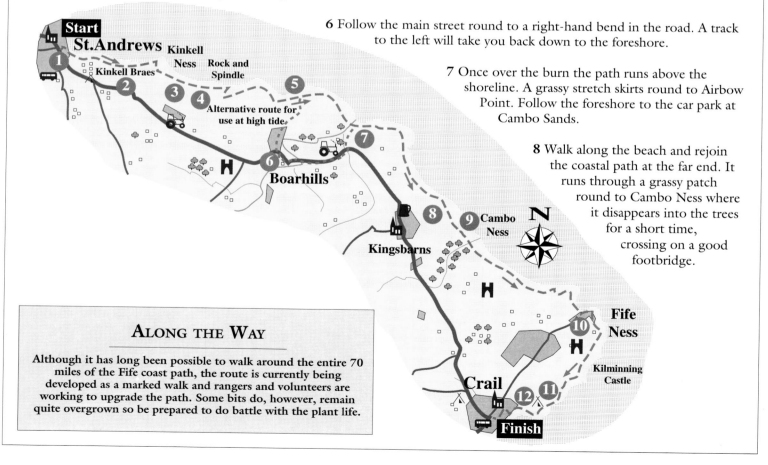

ALONG THE WAY

Although it has long been possible to walk around the entire 70 miles of the Fife coast path, the route is currently being developed as a marked walk and rangers and volunteers are working to upgrade the path. Some bits do, however, remain quite overgrown so be prepared to do battle with the plant life.

The walk ends at the charming fishing village of Crail

9 The path is patchy here, so it's best to follow the beach round; at the next headland it becomes more obvious as it climbs up and round the point. Alternate between foreshore and path until you reach a golf course, then stick to the beach. Keep an eye out for stray golf balls! Below the clubhouse pick up the path again, then a section of road guides you round Fife Ness to the coastguard station.

10 On the roadway just below the lookout the path heads off to the left and rounds the headland to Kilminning Coast Wildlife Reserve. A kissing gate at beach level leads into the reserve and a grassy path runs along the coast to Sauchope caravan park.

11 Walk along the track, through the caravans. Then a stretch of path back from the cliff top leads to Crail and a park which slopes down to one of the town's beaches.

12 Go through the park and before you reach a children's play area, head up to the town. Go left along Nethergate South and then right up Tolbooth Wynd to reach the High Street.

FACT FILE

Distance 13 miles
Time 6 hours
Map OS Landranger 59
Start/parking East Sands, St Andrews, grid ref 517164
Terrain Coastal path, narrow and overgrown in places – make sure you have a pair of long trousers
Nearest town St Andrews
Refreshments Wide choice in St Andrews and Crail

Public transport Fife Scottish bus service from Crail to St Andrews, every hour, on the hour. Adult single around £1.45
Stiles Two
Suitable for All

HARBOURING A SCENIC TREASURE

Visit the picturesque harbour towns and villages of Fife's East Neuk, poetically referred to as a string of pearls draped along the region's coastline.

1 From the centre of Crail, head south-west along the main street (the A917), passing by local shops and above the tiny harbour. Continue past a milestone on the pavement and turn left on to West Braes, a narrow lane heading out towards the coast. It curves right and then left along Osborne Place to pick up the coastal path on the edge of the village.

2 A wooden sign marks the start of the walk proper and a wide gravel path strikes out, passing a fenced compound before dropping down to a grassy bank above the foreshore. Out to sea is the Isle of May, a nature reserve famed for its seabirds. The path is good but becomes dotted with rocks as you approach a boarded-up cottage at The Pans. Beyond this cross a wall and the path continues to Caiplie Caves, an unusual sandstone formation, before passing a renovated farmsteading to arrive in Cellardyke.

3 The approach is through Kilrenny Mills caravan park. Follow the road straight on along The Cooperage, a narrow street of traditional cottages, and continue on Shore Street and then James Street at the next junction into Anstruther. Bear left with the main road into the town centre on the harbourside.

4 A colourful array of fishing boats occupies this safe haven and the Scottish Fisheries Museum is well worth a visit if you have time. A local 'fish supper' is a good bet if you're a bit peckish. Walk along the harbourside and at the far end, before the main road curves right, drop down on to the beach. A few yards on, stepping stones cross the Dreel Burn in the shadow of the church.

5 Once over, climb a short flight of stairs and, turning right, follow a narrow street to link up with the main road again. Follow this up past the Dreel Tavern and take the next road on the left. Turn right in front of Anstruther Wester Primary School and take Shore Road to the local golf club. From there, the coastal path skirts a sandy beach and the golf course and the next port of call, Pittenweem, soon hoves into view.

6 Steps rise up to the edge of the town and a grassy path runs between houses and the cliff top, emerging on to Abbey Wall Road. It curves left, dropping to the harbour. Head along Mid Shore and East Shore to the right of the harbour and continue round the coast to a car park. At the far end a tarmac path meanders along the front of a row of cottages above the beach.

7 At the end of the beach, steps climb up to a play park and from there the coastal path drops down to an outdoor swimming pool before continuing above the beach. A mile further on it reaches St Philip's windmill on the edge of St Monance. Dating from the 18th century and now restored, the mill pumped sea water into adjacent salt pans which have been the subject of recent archaeological investigations. If you want to go inside the mill and view an exhibition within, you have to obtain a key from the newsagent in St Monance.

8 The gravel coastal path borders a park until it reaches a small car park. Follow the road straight ahead to the harbour and continue along the back of the basin to West End, a narrow street crammed with cottages. This way curves right, passing by a short row of houses, and on the left, just beyond a parking area, a narrow flight of steps leads down to the church. Cross a burn and the path skirts left round the large stone wall, using steps cut in the rock.

9 The grassy path rises to dramatic cliff top castle ruins, which can be explored but only with great care. Steps drop down to the foreshore again and the path rises to less impressive castle ruins at Ardross Farm before following a long strip of sandy beach to Elie Ness and the prominent ruin of Lady's Tower, a summerhouse and changing room built for Lady Janet Anstruther in the late 18th century. When you reach the car park above Wood Haven on the edge of Elie, follow the access road inland and at the first junction turn left to reach The Toft. Turn right and it leads up to the centre of the village.

Kilrenny

Anstruther Easter

Anstruther Wester

Pittenweem

St Monance

Elie
Finish

Along the Way

The communities of the East Neuk owe their existence to the sea. The fishing trade is of long standing here and colourful boats of all shapes and sizes still jostle for position in the tiny harbours. Anstruther, Pittenweem and St Monance, which you will visit on this walk, are all working harbour towns. In each you'll find fine examples of the unique architectural style the area is famous for – quaint little cottages with crowstep gables and red pantile roofs, white walls and brightly painted window frames. The sheltered bay of golden sand at Elie attracts watersports enthusiasts from miles around during the summer.

Fact File

Distance 10 miles
Time 5 hours
Map OS Landranger 59
Start Crail town centre, grid ref 613077
Parking Free to north of tourist information centre
Terrain Good coastal path
Nearest town St Andrews
Refreshments Plenty of pubs in Crail, Cellardyke, Anstruther, Pittenweem, St Monance and Elie serving drinks and bar meals

Public transport Fife Scottish bus service number 95 runs hourly from Elie to Crail
Stiles Five
Suitable for All, though dogs are not allowed on any of the harbours

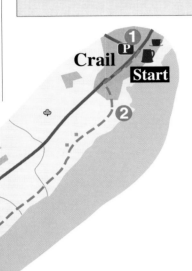

Crail

Start

The harbour at St Monance

THE NORTH

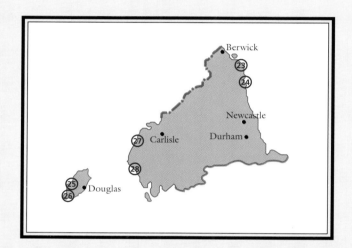

ROCKS, SAND AND SEA AT BAMBURGH

Sea views of the Farne Islands and Holy Island on the outward walk, then lanes,
field paths and tree-clad heights make this a walk of infinite variety.

1 Leave Bamburgh along the Wyndings. At the golf course a sign points you right down to the beach, then turn left and walk round Harkness Rocks and Budle Point into Budle Bay, keeping along the south side.

2 Just before Waren Mill, at a nature reserve sign, go up left to a wicket gate on to the road and turn right. The walk goes left at a sign for Waren House Hotel, but if you want refreshments here continue over the bridge and turn left at the far end of the village.

3 Return to the hotel sign and walk along the country lane, past the hotel for ½ mile to a wicket gate on the left and a sign to Drawkiln Hill. Slant up through the wood, bearing left at the top, to a stile. Two fields follow, then wooded crags and a wall on the left.

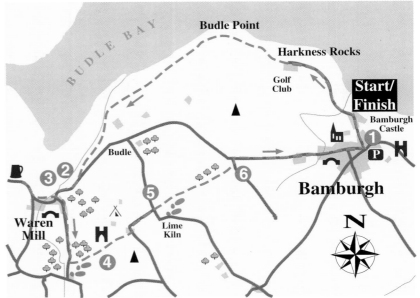

4 Go through a gate at the top and keep just right of a caravan site hedge on the left, ignoring the footpath sign and keeping ahead to a wicket gate on to the road. Turn left. The road bends right and at the junction turn left again.

5 A short distance on is a stone stile and a sign to Bamburgh on the right. Walk along the edge of two fields to a stile. Cross and go ahead up the bank into a third field. Keep a broken wall and then gorse bushes on your left before dropping down to a stile on to a road.

6 Turn left, then right at the next junction to walk back on the wide verge to Bamburgh, passing the church with Grace Darling's tomb and the museum opposite, then on to the castle.

ALONG THE WAY

Check the tides before you set off – the *Newcastle Journal* publishes them every day. If they are not favourable, use one of the many tracks on the dunes between the golf course and the sands to come out at Budle and turn right for Waren Mill. Just before Waren Mill is a nature reserve specializing in sea birds. On the right of the caravan site is a good example of a lime kiln where limestone was burned to spread on the fields. In Bamburgh is the castle, Grace Darling's tomb and museum.

FACT FILE

Distance 6 miles
Time 3 hours
Map O S Landranger 74
Start The Wyndings, a lane opposite the Lord Crewe Arms in the main street, grid ref 349181
Parking Two car parks near the castle; limited parking along the Wyndings, on the dunes

Terrain Easy, though overgrown in parts in summer
Nearest town Bamburgh
Refreshments Pubs, hotels and tea shops in Bamburgh, Burnside Inn at Waren Ford
Public transport Bus service Alnwick-Northumbria 501
Stiles Five
Suitable for Children, dogs, on leads in fields with livestock

KITTIWAKES AND KIPPERS AT CRASTER

Dramatic cliff scenery, a spectacular ruined castle, a wide sandy beach
and field paths make this an outstanding walk.

1 Just inside the Quarry car park are two fingerposts. Follow the one for Craster South Farm, through the trees on the outside of the quarry to a wicket gate into a field and up the slope to a road. Cross into a farm lane at a footpath sign for Howick, past a row of cottages.

2 Go down the lane then through a field to two ladder stiles in the far corner. Cross the one to the right and head slightly right, past two sycamore trees and with the Hips Heugh Crags on your left, aiming for a ladder stile in a wall on the right.

3 Cross it and follow the track over the field, alongside woods to swing up right over a burn on a good track that comes out at the gates of Howick Hall. Turn left and walk along the road for ½ mile to Seahouses, which consists of only a few cottages.

4 The road bends sharp left here. Go ahead through a gate on a green lane to turn left on to the coastal path to Craster, past Sea House, a Victorian cottage with its walls eroded by the salt spray, climbing gently to Cullernose Point.

5 Here the fenced path veers right, then left over the grass to a field gate, then on to a stile where the track is funnelled close to the sea on the

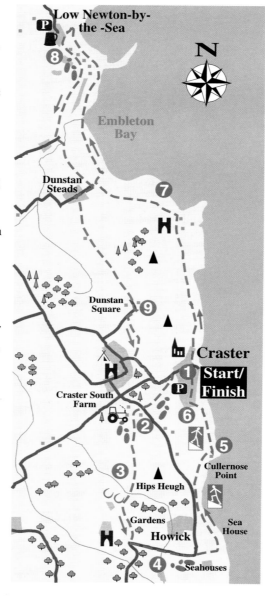

outskirts of Craster. Next it swings up left through a children's playground to the road.

6 Turn right and walk through the village to the harbour. For a short walk, turn up left here and follow the main road back to the car park. For the longer walk, turn right and walk along the front to a wicket gate, then over the grass to Dunstanburgh Castle.

7 Keep to the left of the castle, walking along the edge of the golf course for ½ mile, then cut down on to the beach of Embleton Bay. Turn left and walk 2 miles along to Low Newton-by-the-Sea. Turn up left to the pub and go left in front of it on to the dunes.

8 Pass a pond with hides for watching birds and continue over the dunes. Half a mile along the edge of the golf links, turn up right on a lane to Dunstan Steads. Turn left on a concrete road to Dunstan Square.

9 Follow the road round right past the houses to a sign on the left. Traverse three fields, in the last one going slightly left to a stile on to a road. Cross, turn left and walk back to the car park.

FACT FILE

Distance 10 or 4 miles
Time 4½ or 1½ hours
Maps OS Landrangers 75 and 81
Start/Parking The Quarry car park, Craster, grid ref 256189
Terrain Easy – no hills
Public transport Northumbria Bus Services from Alnwick

Nearest town Alnwick
Refreshments Pubs, hotels in Craster and Bark Pots tea room at the car park
Stiles Three
Suitable for Children, with care on the cliff section and on the road from Howick to Seahouses, which can be unexpectedly busy. Dogs, on lead where sheep in fields

ALONG THE WAY

The gardens at Howick Hall are well worth a visit, especially in spring, and seabirds nest in the high basalt cliffs at Cullernose Point and Dunstanburgh Castle, open to the public. These are all part of the great Whin Sill that slants south-west across Northumberland and upon which Hadrian's Wall is built. Craster is famous for its kippers and the smokehouse can be seen on the village street opposite the Jolly Fisherman.

THROUGH THE WILD GLEN

Two of the Isle of Man's waymarked trails are conveniently sampled in a short walk around Glen Maye and Glen Rushen.

1 Park in Glenmaye village close to the entrance to Glen Maye. A stepped path descends into the deep, dark, wooded confines of the glen, then a footbridge allows a fine view of a waterfall. Continue down through the glen, noting the 'wheel pit' of a former waterwheel. Turn left along a track leading to the very end of the glen. Turn left to follow a path up a brackeny slope above the shore and continue through fields. The path leads on to a main road at Ballachrink.

2 Turn right along the road and follow it for a mile to the village of Dalby. There is a pub at this point, or you can continue straight onwards to leave the village. Watch for a narrow road on the right, which descends to a small river. Look out for a track climbing up from the river and out on to a more open lane. Don't take the first footpath signposted for the coast on the right, but take the one at a higher level, which is marked as part of the Raad ny Foillan.

3 This path descends in loops on a rugged slope, then runs more gently downhill to cross the ravine of Glion Mooar. Once you have crossed this the path climbs uphill from the cliffs, then you turn left along a more prominent track. Follow this past the isolated Eary Cushlin, and along the top side of Kerroodhoo Plantation to reach a main road.

4 Turn right along the road, then left at a gateway marked as the Bayr ny Skeddan. Follow the track into Glen Rushen, passing another gateway into a forest. You will notice a pathway leading off to the right which descends into Glen Mooar. Note the mining remains on the hillside above before you cross the river and turn left along a good, clear track. The track joins a road near the Arrasey Plantation.

5 The road through the forest is barred to vehicles, so you will have it all to yourself as you continue down through Glen Mooar. Look out for a map board on the left further on, which indicates the short line of the Postman's Walk. This leads down to the river, crosses it using a footbridge, then you have a choice of two quite short paths. Both later join roads where you need to turn right, and you will be led straight back into the village of Glenmaye.

FACT FILE

Distance 8 miles
Time 4–5 hours
Maps OS Landranger 95. Isle of Man Public Rights of Way and Outdoor Leisure Map
Start/parking Glenmaye, grid ref 235797
Terrain Good paths, tracks and roads by woods, fields and cliffs
Nearest town Peel
Refreshments Pubs in Glenmaye and Dalby
Public transport Isle of Man Transport, tel 01624 662525
Stiles A few, but not difficult for dogs
Suitable for Older children and dogs on leads

ALONG THE WAY

The Raad ny Foillan, or Gull's Road, is a waymarked coastal footpath encircling the Isle of Man. The Bayr ny Skeddan, or Herring Way, is a waymarked coast-to-coast footpath crossing the island. They meet in Glen Maye, which is one of a series of lovely, wooded Manx National Glens. The route starts with a charming waterfall walk and continues along the coastal footpath.

Waterfall in beautiful Glen Maye

ROUND THE SOUND

The southern end of the Isle of Man is fringed with dramatic cliffs bearing a fine coastal footpath.

1 Starting at the harbour at Port St Mary, follow Clifton Road around Kallow Point. You can leave the road and walk just seawards of it, then follow a path climbing up a flight of steps alongside a golf course. When you reach Fistard Road turn left and cross a bridge, then climb steeply uphill and follow the road until it becomes a track which leads to a gateway.

2 The Raad ny Foillan, or coastal footpath, continues through the fields. You will need to drift uphill later to keep above the cliffs overlooking the Sugarloaf. Spend time watching the gulls wheeling around, then proceed past the Chasms. This deeply fissured ground looks most interesting, but you are reminded to be careful if you want to explore it in detail. A nearby derelict café provides handy shelter.

3 Continue walking along the coastal footpath, which is surrounded by ground-hugging gorse scrub and heather. As you work your way around Bay Stacka, look out for a left turn where a path leads to Black Head. Spanish Head and Burroo Ned follow – the last headland bearing a promontory fort. The Calf of Man is well displayed out to sea, and when you reach the Sound you will find a handy café. Boat trips are sometimes run to the Calf of Man, where a flock of Manx Loaghtan Sheep and profuse birdlife can be studied.

4 Leaving the Sound, the Raad ny Foillan is blazed around a series of rocky headlands, and you may find seaward views are graced by the distant profile of the Mountains of Mourne. The coastal footpath wanders around Fine Bay, then finally reaches a point above Port Erin. On the descent, you follow a tall wall across a slope, then descend via steps alongside a Marine Biological Station. Follow the harbourside into Port Erin, a pleasant little town with full facilities.

5 You could catch a bus or steam train from Port Erin to Port St Mary, but a short road walk would quickly close the distance between them. You could either follow Station Road and turn right at the roundabout to reach Port St Mary, or follow St Mary's Road and Truggan Road for a quieter backroad return.

FACT FILE

Distance 8 miles
Time 4–5 hours
Maps OS Landranger 95. Isle of Man Public Rights of Way and Outdoor Leisure Map
Start Port St Mary, grid ref 212673
Parking Port St Mary, the Sound and Port Erin
Terrain Fairly easy cliff paths, though surrounded by rugged ground
Nearest towns Port St Mary and Port Erin
Refreshments Port St Mary, The Sound and Port Erin

Public transport Isle of Man Transport, tel 01624 662525
Stiles A few, but not too difficult for dogs
Suitable for Older children and dogs on leads. Disabled people could wander around the Sound, or visit the Folk Museum just inland at Cregneash

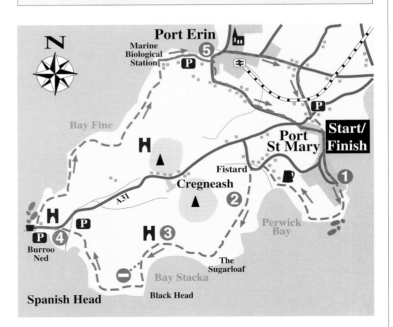

ALONG THE WAY

Port St Mary and Port Erin have almost filled the narrow neck of low-lying ground at the southern end of the Isle of Man. Just beyond these small towns, however, are rugged and precipitous cliffs which are home to a wide variety of birds. The Raad ny Foillan, or Gull's Road, is an apt name for the coastal footpath which runs all around the Isle of Man. This short stretch is one of the best parts. The first half passes through a large Manx National Trust holding. Cliff formations include the Sugarloaf, the fissures known as the Chasms, and the treacherous water-washed rocks around the Calf Sound.

The harbour at Port Erin, reached at point 5

ROMAN REMAINS

Follow in the footsteps of the Romans along the coast of north-west Cumbria, enjoying grand views across to the Isle of Man and over the Solway to Galloway.

1 Set off from the car park and cross the bridge over the River Ellen, enjoying a fine view of the picturesque houses that line North Quay. Ahead lies the Maritime Museum, housed above the tourist information office. Both are well worth a visit. Cross Senhouse Street and continue along King Street, keeping to the right of Christ Church. Join the promenade as soon as you can for a bracing walk, with a magnificent view of the Solway estuary and across to towering Criffel and the lesser hills of southern Scotland. Continue past the children's play area and then look for an unsignposted gap in the concrete wall on your right. Beyond, a narrow path leads gently up the Sea Brows – old sandstone cliffs – to join a tarmacked footpath. Turn right and continue to the Senhouse Roman Museum.

2 To continue the walk, return to the tarmacked path and walk right (north) along the cliffs. Pass below several quarried areas and follow the path as it gradually descends to join the promenade. Below, on the sands, waders and gulls probe for food. Just before the farm at the end of the cliffs, Bank End (1761), turn right to walk a reinforced path, passing to the right of the buildings. Stride on past the golf course clubhouse and continue to the A596, which you cross. Turn right and walk the few yards to the start of the cemetery. Pass through the signposted gate and walk ahead, with the high wall of the graveyard to your right. Follow the wall round until you come to a hedge, then go beside it uphill to the boundary. Turn left and walk ahead, passing through four gates. From this high-level way you have spectacular views of Skiddaw and the Buttermere mountains to your right and the sea to your left.

3 Beyond the fourth gate, stride the hedged track towards Crosby. At the end of the track, to your left, you can see the attractive church of St John's, Crosscanonby, which you might like to visit to see its Viking hogback gravestone. Turn right to walk into Crosby. At the T junction, cross the road and walk left. At the village green turn right to follow the public footpath sign directing you through Hill Farm. Just before a new bungalow, take the gate on the right behind the farm, where you are asked to keep all dogs on leads.

4 Walk ahead over four pastures – the stiled way is easy to follow. Cross the farm track by two stiles and then continue down the hedge on your right to another. Strike half left to another stile near the left corner of the pasture. Continue in the same direction to cross a stile in the opposite boundary. Walk beside the fence on your left to a signposted gate on to a narrow lane. Turn left and walk the flower-lined way to cross the West Coast railway line and then Dereham bridge over the River Ellen.

5 Continue on to take the footpath on the right, signposted Maryport. Here curlews fill the air with their haunting calls. Walk the stiled way to drop downhill to a waymarked post, where you walk left along a sunken track. This leads to the side of the river. Walk left, downstream, along the lovely riverside path, through woodland which in spring is carpeted with kingcups, celandines, butterbur, wood anemones, wood sorrel, woodrush and primroses.

6 Follow the clear path out of the trees. Continue above the woodland and then descend to the side of the railway line and the river again. Keep to the right of the houses ahead to walk a track to the A594. Cross the road and bear right. Climb up Wood Street, where at the top you have a grand view over the harbour. Descend Brow Steps, turn left and cross the bridge to rejoin your car.

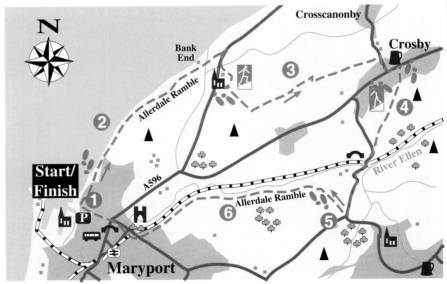

FACT FILE

Distance 8 miles
Time 4–5 hours
Maps OS Landranger 89, OS Pathfinder 575 NY 03/13
Start/parking South Quay pay-and-display car park, grid ref 033366
Terrain Easy walking all the way, though the path by the river can be muddy after rain
Nearest town Maryport
Refreshments Plenty of cafés and pubs in Maryport; drinks, sweets and ices at the museum
Public transport By rail link from Carlisle and Barrow-in-Furness
Stiles Many, varied, all easy
Suitable for Children, dogs on leads

ALONG THE WAY

Maryport is named after Mary, wife of Humphrey Senhouse the second, a landowner who began to develop the area in the 1700s. The Senhouse family began the collection of Roman remains now on display in the museum that bears their name. Alauna, the fort adjacent to the museum, was the headquarters garrison of Hadrian's coastal defence system, which extended northwards to Bowness-on-Solway. In 1870, 17 Roman altars were dug up. Today the collection is housed in the remodelled drill hall, known as the Battery, built in 1885. Fletcher Christian, of Mutiny on the Bounty fame, was born nearby.

Once the Maryport docks handled vast quantities of cargo but they have since silted up and the old dock area has been pleasingly developed.

This walk provides far-reaching views across the Solway to southern Scotland

HIGH DRAMA

This lovely coastal walk, which requires a head for heights, climbs sandstone cliffs,
visits a lonely bay and passes close to a lighthouse.

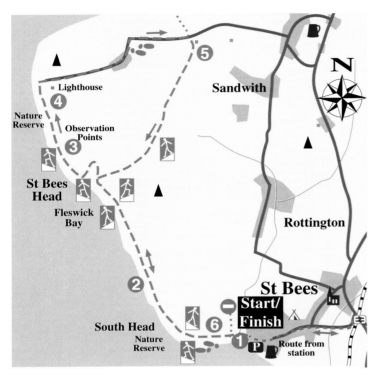

4 There is one more platform to visit and then a short stroll brings you to a small building housing the foghorn. Turn left before it and join a metalled road to the lighthouse, which was built in 1822. Follow the metalled road beyond it into the surrounding countryside, passing between farm outbuildings and in front of two houses.

5 Where the road swings sharply to the left, look for a covered reservoir on the right. Leave the lane, taking a track on the right that runs beside the reservoir. Climb a ladder stile and continue to the next one. Walk on to a gate ahead. Beyond, continue beside the wall on your left, dropping steadily downhill until you reach a stile at the head of the ravine leading down to Fleswick. From here return left along the cliff path to St Bees.

6 On your way to the station, or as you drive away from the beach, you might still have time to visit the church, with its striking tower and fine arch over the west door. Set among flowering grasses in the churchyard is a small stone pillar with ornate patterning, the base of a Viking Cross.

1 If starting from the station, walk left and take a signposted footpath across St Bees public school playing field. Continue towards the sea. Bear right to pass through the large car park, where you start if you've travelled by car. Continue to the end of the promenade. Cross Rottington Beck by footbridge and follow the signpost for the Head. Climb the steep slope through the low-growing vegetation and then go on for 2 miles along the narrow path of rich red soil.

2 Cross the next two stiles and follow the path as it gently descends through a meadow and then follow steps down to the ravine below. Clamber left over the wide smooth sandstone boulders to the beach at Fleswick Bay. To the north of the bay, rearing upwards, stands the magnificent St Bees Head. Return along the ravine and cross the stile over a wire fence on the left. Climb the slope, pausing to look back at the secluded beach.

3 The first railed observation point lies over a stile to the left. It provides a magnificent view of a huge cliff face where fulmars, kittiwakes, guillemots and black guillemots breed. Make your way on to the second and then the third observation point – from here you can look out across the sea to the Isle of Man. To the north lie the hills of Galloway. From the next platform you might see puffins far below on a wide ledge.

FACT FILE

Distance 6½ miles from the car park or 8 miles from the railway station
Time 3–4 hours
Map OS Landranger 89
Start/parking Promenade car park, St Bees, grid ref 961118
Terrain Distinct cliff paths, some close to cliff edge. Some lane walking, virtually traffic-free
Nearest town Whitehaven
Refreshments Café and inn in the village, hotel on the promenade
Public transport Trains run from Carlisle (tel 01228 44711) and from Barrow-in-Furness (tel 01229 820805) and intermediate stations. Buses run from Whitehaven and Egremont but services are infrequent, tel 01946 592000
Stiles Eight, all easy
Suitable for Accompanied children. Dogs on leads

ALONG THE WAY

St Bees Head, where Alfred Wainwright started his Coast to Coast Walk, entices many walkers away from the Lakeland tops. Leave yourself time to explore the beach at Fleswick to look for semi-precious stones and visit the cave at the northern end, once the haunt of smugglers. Above all take your binoculars and use the birdwatching observation points to look in on the activity on the ledges of the cliffs. Finally, round the day off with a visit to the village and its Priory Church, which has a fine Norman arch over the west door.

Magnificent St Bees Head rears up above Fleswick Bay

YORKSHIRE, HUMBERSIDE AND THE NORTH WEST

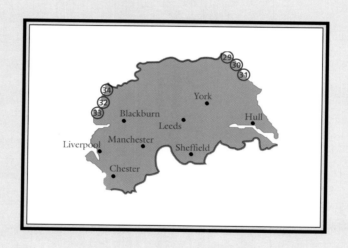

PAST REFLECTIONS

Hidden among the towering cliffs of North Yorkshire are quaint old villages where time has stood still. Visit two of them on this walk.

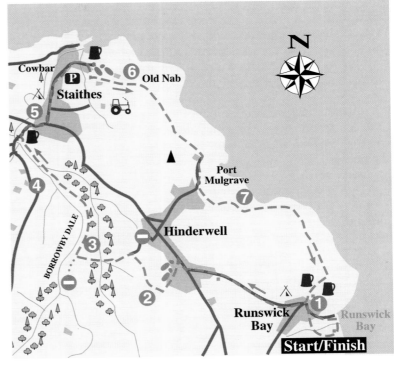

1 From the cliff top car park turn left towards Hinderwell. As you enter Hinderwell bear right past the war memorial. Cross the road, then in 50yds turn left along a wide path, signed as a footpath, alongside house number 98. Keep straight ahead, then cross a stile into a field.

2 Leave the field via a stile, and bear right into a muddy lane. The lane soon bears right, then after a long straight section it turns sharp right. You turn left here over a stile at the sign asking you to keep to the path. Cross the field to another stile, then turn right downhill. Cross a stile into the wood and you soon reach a stream.

3 Cross a footbridge over the stream, then climb steeply up the other side to a field. Keep straight ahead, following a well-worn path through the corn into a wood. As you enter the wood, take the path on the right. Keep straight ahead, passing a yellow waymark, then exit over a stile on to a wide grassy path.

4 Pass a stile without a fence and continue to a steep incline. Cross a stile into a caravan site. Leave the site through a gate and turn right over the bridge at the sign for Dalehouse. When you reach the road go right up the hill past the Fox & Hounds pub to the main road. Turn right, then in a few yards cross the road and turn left at the sign for 'Staithes ½ mile'.

5 At the mini-roundabout keep straight ahead, then walk down the steep hill into Old Staithes. Head along the cobbled street, eventually arriving at the Cod & Lobster pub and harbour. Turn right here along Church Street and walk uphill, following a sign for the coast path. When the cobbles end keep straight ahead on to a narrow track, following signs for the Cleveland Way.

6 Pass the farm, then follow the coast path across fields and three stiles to a fence. Go right to a stile at the top of the hill. Keep on the cliff path and take the diversion as marked to the road at Port Mulgrave. Cross a stile and go past a few houses, then when the road turns right to the village you turn left on to the cliff path, following the Cleveland Way sign.

7 Follow the cliff path, taking great care as it is eroded in places. Pass over 4 stiles. After about 2 miles turn right to cross a stile at the yellow waymark. This takes you over a field to the road. Cross the road, following the sign for Runswick Bay Beach down a steep hill. After exploring Runswick Bay follow the narrow road at the sign for the Royal Hotel, towards the red telephone kiosk. At the Royal Hotel take the steps in front of you to climb the cliff. When you reach a small road turn right to continue up the cliff. The path takes you back to the car park.

FACT FILE

Distance 7 miles
Time 3 hours
Maps OS Landranger 94, OS outdoor Leisure 27
Start/parking Runswick Bay cliff top car park, grid ref 808161
Terrain Good woodland paths. Cliff paths generally good but some erosion causing the path to be near the edge of the high cliffs between Port Mulgrave and Runswick Bay
Nearest town Whitby
Refreshments Pubs at Dalehouse, Staithes and Runswick Bay. Cafés at Staithes and Runswick Bay
Public transport Service from Middlesborough and Whitby by Tees Buses, tel 01947 602146
Stiles eighteen
Suitable for All, but keep children and animals under close supervision along the cliff paths

ALONG THE WAY

Tiny fishing communities sprang up along the Yorkshire coast many years ago. Some now cater for the holiday trade, but fishing still plays a part in the two villages on this route. Staithes reflects life as it was 100 years ago. Look for the Coble boats tied up in neat rows along the harbour side, the Bethel Mission house, old cobbled streets, narrow ginnels between the houses and mysterious old pubs, where echoes of long ago still linger.

FROM ABBEY TO ARTISTS

This glorious 12-mile circular walk traverses the route of the disused Scarborough to Whitby railway and returns you along the magnificent Heritage Coast.

1 From the car park, walk south and go on to climb Spital Hill. Cross the A171 with care, and continue ahead along Larpool Lane, past the cemetery and some houses into the pleasing countryside. Pass beneath a disused railway bridge and take the stepped path that climbs right to the start of the dismantled railway path. Now the walk has really begun.

2 The cinder-covered way continues for 5½ miles to the edge of Robin Hood's Bay. Pass alongside Cock Mill Wood, then continue by the outskirts of the villages of Stainsacre and Hawsker and on into the quiet seclusion of rural Yorkshire. At the gated end of the track, follow the waymarks left.

3 Here you might like to visit Robin Hood's Bay, a small picturesque fishing village which is a mecca for artists, with its jumble of red-roofed houses. There is a steep descent to the seashore – and a steep ascent to start your return to Whitby.

4 To continue the walk, return to the last waymark and take the grassy track leading north, signposted Cleveland Way. It passes several houses and then through dense blackthorn bushes crowding the cliff top. Head on into Rocket Post Field. Sit on the second bench seat and enjoy the magnificent view of the fishing village.

5 From here a distinct stiled path continues all the way to Whitby, giving you breathtaking views of the fine coastline and the seemingly endless North Sea. The fenced way descends into and out of stepped hollows. At Maw Wyke Hole watch the fulmars nesting on the inaccessible ledges of the cliffs. Cross Oakham Beck, where the Coast-to-Coast walk joins the Cleveland Way. After another stepped hollow the

path moves outside the fence and along the edge of a 300-foot perpendicular cliff. Take care here, particularly in windy weather and if walking with children.

6 Look out for the waymarked stile that gives access to a path that passes on the landward side of Whitby lighthouse. Cross the access road and take the stiled path to a ladder stile on the seaward side of Whitby Fog Signal. Continue on past Black Nab and Saltwick Bay, then follow the Cleveland Way signs through Whitby Holiday Village and bear right to the cliff edge to walk the reinforced fenced track.

7 Go on to pass the coastguard station. Beyond, on the left, lie the famous Abbey ruins, which are well worth a visit. Stroll past St Mary's Church; its churchyard is the setting for part of the story of Dracula, by Bram Stoker. Continue down the 199 steps, immortalised by Stoker, to Church Street. Walk ahead to return to your car.

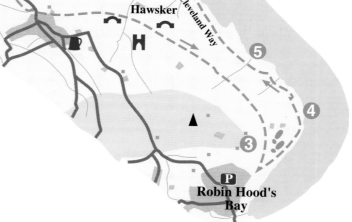

The dramatic ruins of Whitby Abbey can be seen on the skyline above the town

ALONG THE WAY

The fishing port of Whitby is set within a cleft in the north-east Yorkshire coast. At the base of the cleft flows the River Esk, and the red pantiled houses of the quaint town climb the cliffs on both sides of its mouth. Leave time at either end of your walk for a wander through this lovely town, which is packed with historical interest.

Once a pet polar bear roamed in Cock Mill Wood, having escaped from captivity. It had been brought back from the Arctic by William Scoresby, a whaler, who kept it as a pet instead of having it killed for its oil.

FACT FILE

Distance 12 miles
Time 7 hours
Maps OS Landranger 94, OS Outdoor Leisure 27
Start/parking Pay-and-display car park beside the Fleece Inn, overlooking the River Esk in Church Street (east bank of the river), grid ref 902109
Terrain Easy walking for most of the way
Nearest town Whitby
Refreshments Good choice in Whitby and Robin Hood's Bay
Public transport Yorkshire Coastliner, tel 01653 692556
Stiles Several along the cliff top, standard type
Suitable for Energetic walkers and dogs on leads.

CLIFFS AND RAILWAYS

The Cleveland Way affords superb seascapes of the Yorkshire Coast as it runs along the edge of the cliffs from Robin Hood's Bay to Ravenscar. The track-bed of the Scarborough to Whitby railway, now disused, provides a pleasing tree-lined return on this eight-mile circular walk.

1 From the car park walk down the very steep narrow road into the delightful fishing village, where you will want to linger. Leave the village by any stepped track that climbs south, passing through steeply wooded banks out on to the cliffs. Walk the well waymarked Cleveland Way, which is initially reinforced.

2 Enjoy the fine views back to the village and ahead to the 600-foot cliffs of Ravenscar and the dramatic crenellated walls of the Raven Hall Hotel. Walk on and then descend the long flight of steps into Boggle Hole, where Mill Beck emerges from its rocky wooded ravine. The youth hostel (Bay Mill until 1928) stands in this leafy hollow. The slopes of the little bay were supposed to be haunted by a boggle, or goblin.

3 Climb the long flight of steps out of the hollow and continue along the Cleveland Way. This leads to a footbridge deep in another hollow over the Stoupe Beck. Cross a narrow road. Take the signposted path on the left. If the tide is low, look down to the left to see the crescent-shaped reefs.

4 Continue on the fine coastal walk, which veers inland to continue along a reinforced cart track. Watch for the waymark that directs you to the right fork where the track branches. At the next branch take the left fork. Continue to the tiny hamlet of Ravenscar, where you might like to visit St Hilda's Church at the south end of the village.

5 Return to the Cleveland Way and walk back (west) for 100 yards. Turn left to join the disused railway track. This glorious route continues for 4 miles, passing below many interesting bridges and a viaduct. It comes close to the old Brickyard Alum Quarry, where alum shale was burnt and then leached before alum crystals were produced. The material was used for fixing dyes, tanning leather and manufacturing candles and parchment. Later, bricks were produced on the site.

6 After passing through the gate to the road at Robin Hood's Bay, turn right, then cross and follow the waymarked track to pass the old station buildings to the car park.

FACT FILE

Distance 8 miles
Time 4 hours
Maps OS Outdoor Leisure 27, OS Landranger 94
Start/parking Station car park, Robin Hood's Bay, grid ref 949055
Terrain Easy walking for most of the way but there are precipitous stepped climbs and descents. After rain expect plenty of mud along the Cleveland Way. Stout footwear essential
Nearest town Whitby
Refreshments Cafés in Robin Hood's Bay
Public transport Tees and District buses 93, 93A Middlesbrough-Whitby-Scarborough. Tel 01947 602146
Stiles Two, both easy
Suitable for Energetic families and dogs under close control

ALONG THE WAY

If the tide is out look down to the beach for a spectacular view of the great crescent-shaped reefs, or scars as they are known locally, evidence of the tremendous eroding power of the North Sea. Ravenscar is known as the resort that never was. Once named Peak, it was laid out with sites for houses and shops, but – fortunately or unfortunately according to your preferences – the entrepreneur ran out of money and the area was not developed. When the railway arrived it was renamed Ravenscar.

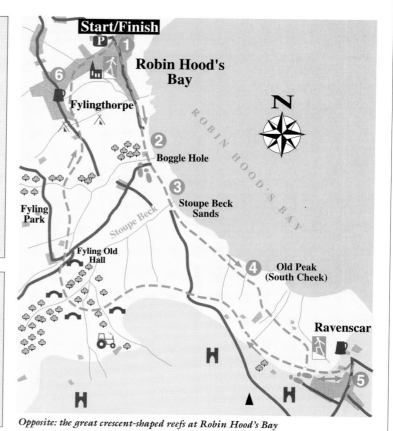

Opposite: the great crescent-shaped reefs at Robin Hood's Bay

COASTAL RELICS

From Cockerham pass the atmospheric remains of an abbey and finish at a church with its solid tower and plague gravestones.

1 Walk north to pass in front of the Manor Inn and continue to a turning on the right. This is Willy Lane, a bridleway signposted Ellel Grange. Follow the track as it swings left towards a farm called Up Town and then right just before the dwelling. At the end of the short track bear left to pass through a gate behind a pylon. Strike diagonally right across the corner of the field to pass through a gate. Drop down the slope to cross two footbridges and then swing left beside a wood.

2 Take the first gate into a wide grassy area between two sections of the wood. Pass in front of Ellel Grange and go through a gate to the right of Home Farm. A gate opposite gives access to parkland. Continue to a gate ahead and then walk diagonally left to come close to Double Bridge. Continue left, close to the thorn hedge, to reach a squeezer stile to the junction of the canal with the Glasson branch at Junction Bridge number 1.

3 Cross the cobbled turnover bridge and turn left to follow the towpath for 2½ miles to the Glasson Basin. Look for Thurnham Hall away on the left after the fifth bridge over the waterway. In Glasson pause as you cross the swing bridge – to the left is the canal basin, used as a marina, and to the right the dock, where ocean-going boats are loaded.

4 Walk up Tithebarn Hill and pause to catch your breath and to enjoy the magnificent view. Follow the road left and at the crossroads turn right to walk along an enclosed lane that passes a caravan site. Go through the gate beyond and walk with a shrubby hawthorn hedge on your right. Follow it as it bears left. Cross a gated footbridge and then pass to the left of Crook Farm. Follow the farm's access track left and as you go, if the tide is on the way in, watch the myriad seabirds hunting for prey on the ever-decreasing area of sand.

5 Where the farm road swings inland, continue along the shore to pass Abbey Lighthouse cottage beside its lighthouse. Beyond the next stile continue along the breakwater to come to Cockersands Abbey. Go on, with the marsh and Cocker Channel to your right. Continue past the caravan site and on to Bank End Farm, where you join a road. Go along it beside a high embankment to its end and turn right to walk towards Pattys Farm and the Black Knights parachute centre.

6 Just before the farm cross the stile on to higher ground on the left and continue to a stiled footbridge on the right, which you cross. Pass through the gate in the left corner and continue with the ditch to your left, through gates and over footbridges to join the road.

7 Turn left and follow the gated, paved path on the right to visit St Michael's church. Beyond, take the wide reinforced track back to Cockerham parish hall.

Double Bridge on the Lancaster Canal with its middle wall which serves as a boundary between two farms

FACT FILE

Distance 10 miles
Time 5 hours
Map OS Landranger 102
Start/parking Cockerham village hall, grid ref 465521
Terrain Easy walking – muddy farm tracks after rain
Nearest towns Lancaster, Garstang
Refreshments Manor Inn, Cockerham. Cafés and pubs in Glasson
Public transport Buses from Preston to Lancaster, tel 01524 84656
Stiles Eight, all easy
Suitable for Children, dogs on leads

ALONG THE WAY

Zip up your fleece for this breezy walk with glimpses of the area's past. The bracing wind that accompanies you across Cockerham Sands buffets the tower of St Michael's. Double Bridge on the Lancaster Canal is double the width of other canal bridges and has a wall along the middle that forms a boundary between two farms. Colourful Glasson was developed when the River Lune silted up in the 1780s and ships were unable to reach St George's Quay in Lancaster. The abbey was built in 1190 on what was once a small island, the site of an earlier hospital that housed lepers.

CIRCULAR WALK FROM PILLING MARSH

This tour takes you along the embankment overlooking Pilling Marsh and Preesall Sands, and then beside the silvery estuary of the River Wyre, returning you along the embankment, with a grand view of the Bleasdale Fells and the Lakeland mountains.

1 From the bus stop, walk the lane to the large parking area and up on to the embankment. There is limited parking on the embankment as well, so get there early if you wish to do some extra birdwatching in comfort! Follow the Lancashire coastal way arrow pointing to the left (west). Look for a variety of birds in the willow-edged ponds to the left as you dawdle to the stile, enjoying the superb view across the marsh and sands. Beyond the stile, the right of way drops down left and continues ahead below the embankment – a good place to be if a fearsome wind is coming off the sea. In spring this sheltered way hosts many skylarks and the air is full of their sweet songs.

2 At the signpost, turn inland to climb two stiles and then cross a pasture to a narrow road. Turn right and go on to pass Fluke Hall, a fine house set among tall beeches that shadow a pool. Continue to Fluke Hall parking area to rejoin the glorious embankment, where huge limestone boulders have been piled high as part of the sea defence. Continue on into Knott End and along the esplanade to the car park behind Knott End Café, once the terminus for the 'Pilling Pig', the old Garstang to Knott End railway. This is your point of arrival if you have taken the ferry across the Wyre.

3 Walk upstream of the river along the signposted footpath, with the pleasing skyline of Fleetwood across the water. Just before Sea Dyke Cottage (1754), turn left away from the estuary path. Turn right behind the dwelling to follow the footpath right, along the edge of the golf course. Waymarks direct you diagonally across the links to join a farm track. Continue right, past a pond, and then left (arrowed) into Whinny Lane (a track). Stroll through woodland to pass the Jacobean Hackensall Hall and carry on, ignoring all side paths.

4 At a wide junction of tracks, turn right to walk the track-bed of the old railway to Hall Gate Lane. Turn right, cross Ford Stones Bridge and head on into the village of Preesall, passing the Black Bull and the

Saracen's Head on your right. Turn left into Smithy Lane and left again in front of Preesall's Charity School. Turn left once more, behind the garage of the house on your left, to walk the winding fenced path around the school's nature trail. Enjoy the splendid views of the Fylde Plain and the Forest of Bowland beyond.

5 Before the end of the fenced way, take a stile on your left and descend to a footbridge over a ditch. Stride on to cross two more stiles and then a ladder stile to a road, which you cross. Turn left and then right into Gaulter's Lane. At the end of the lane, and before a gate, turn left to walk a signposted narrow strip of grass close to a ditch. Beyond the kissing gate, cross on a right diagonal to a footbridge. Beyond, walk ahead to a stile close to two hawthorns then continue between two fishing ponds (Boubles Ponds), where you turn left.

6 Carry on until you come to another pond, where you bear right into the gated and stiled Tongues Lane, a private lane with footpath access. Go on past a duck farm where the lane swings right, round the end of the pens, walk ahead along a signposted footpath, with a ditch to your left. Follow the stiled way to Pilling Lane, which you cross. Pass through the stone stile and walk ahead along the stiled way to rejoin the esplanade.

7 Turn right and stroll along, with pleasing views ahead. At Fluke Hall, just before tall pines, leave the embankment and walk the narrow lane to pass Fluke Hall. Continue to the signposted stile, on the left, to cross the pasture. Beyond the stiles, turn right and continue to the Lane Ends amenity area.

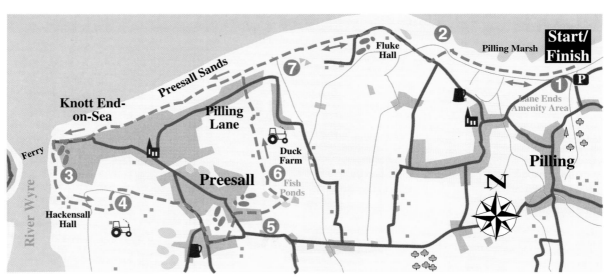

Distance 11½ miles
Time 4–5 hours
Map OS Landranger 102
Start/parking At the landscaped parking area, Lane Ends Amenity Area, just off the A588, grid ref 415495
Terrain A long level walk, easy going underfoot
Nearest towns Lancaster, Preston
Refreshments Saracen's Head and Black Bull at Preesall; café at Knott End car park
Public transport Town Bus 89 Lancaster–Knott End (best service non-school days and Saturdays), alight at Lane Ends. Tel 01524 32878. Tram from Blackpool–Fleetwood and then cross the River Wyre by ferry – start walk at Knott End car park
Stiles Many but none difficult
Suitable for All. January to Good Friday no dogs allowed on a small part of the embankment walk. At other times all dogs on leads.

ALONG THE WAY

Sheep close-graze the embankment and the marsh, sharing them with shelducks, redshanks, curlews, oyster catchers, green plovers, innumerable gulls and long-legged hares. The inland part of the walk traverses what was formerly a huge peat bog, once thought to be bottomless. The Duke of Hamilton, who owned much of the area, drained it, using miles of pipes made at his own tile works to create arable land.

The limestone boulders on the embankment at Knott End form part of the sea defences

VILLAGE BY THE SEA

Walk through fields and coastal marshes to the quaint village of Sunderland, enjoying fantastic views across Morecambe Bay on your return.

1 From the Globe Hotel car park, turn right down the lane marked cul-de-sac and continue ahead to the fork. Bear left at the fork and then take the ladder stile on the right, signed 'Public footpath, Carr Lane, Middleton'. Cross the ladder stile and continue across the field. Climb the next ladder stile and walk across the next field, heading for the signpost that you can see ahead of you. Cross this next stile, walk across the field, go over a small stile and walk ahead over a large field, with Heysham power station to the right and the Lune to the left. Head for the farthest corner of the field, cross the stile and continue in the same direction with the hedgerow close to your left. Climb the next ladder stile and continue straight ahead over another stile; walk on up the farm track until you meet a country lane.

2 Walk left down the lane, following it around several bends, until it ends. Turn left along the beach, following a bridleway signed Sunderland Point. Walk on through the next three gateways, continuing in the same direction with the foreshore to your right. Immediately before reaching the pond climb the wattle fencing and continue along the shoreline, heading in the same direction. Continue to Sambo's grave.

3 From here retrace your steps about 130 paces to the sign for the bridleway on your right. Go through the gate and up the tiny path. When you reach its end continue along the lane towards the road. Just before a T junction note Upstairs Cottage, where Sambo died, on the left. It can be identified by the stairs on the outside. Turn left along the village road and soon after passing the public toilets, climb the ladder stile and walk to the right along the sea wall. Continue for a long way along the top of this flood barrier until the footpath drops down over a fence on to a country lane. Turn right and head back to the Globe

FACT FILE

Distance 5 miles
Time 2 hours
Map OS Landranger 102
Start/parking Car park, Globe Hotel, Overton, grid ref 434579
Terrain Mostly distinct paths and some country lanes
Nearest town Heysham
Refreshments Numerous in Overton
Public transport None
Stiles Numerous
Suitable for Children

ALONG THE WAY

The quiet village of Sunderland is at times very remote indeed – at high tides vehicular access to it is cut off due to flooding of the road. In 1735 a young West Indian boy called Sambo died in Upstairs Cottage in Sunderland. He had been employed as a servant of a sea captain before catching a fever. Being black he was denied a burial in consecrated ground and was instead interred in a far-flung corner of the parish, looking out to sea. Be sure to visit the isolated grave and read the inscription on the sad tomb that lies in this lonely spot.

Remote and peaceful Sunderland Point

LINCOLNSHIRE AND EAST ANGLIA

SEA BREEZES

Fortify yourself with the sea air as you walk through the dunes on the east coast.

1 From the car park, face the sea and take the circular tour of the nature reserve on the right by following the well-laid-out paths and information boards. Then enter the sand dunes by climbing the steps to the top of the hillock and follow any one of the trails in a north-westerly direction along the dunes. From the ridge top on the right is a great view of the saltmarsh which is regularly covered by the sea. The plants that grow here survive despite being covered by saltwater and dried out by the wind. Marsh samphire is particularly common here – vast quantities used to be gathered and burnt to make soda for the manufacture of soap and glass. Over to the left on the horizon are the hills of the Lincolnshire Wolds.

Sand dunes around Saltfleet

2 When the path meets the corner of Sea View Farm, climb the stile on the right and re-enter the dunes. Follow the track by the side of the fence to a white gate and another small car park. Alternatively climb the sand dune and make your way through to the same point, but your legs will need to be well protected against the sea buckthorn. Continue from the car park through the dunes. When you reach two stiles climb the double-stepped one on the right and head towards the white-topped domed mill at Saltfleet. At the end of the fence line, descend into a hollow and, at the fork, go either right or left to a concrete bridge with a metal sluice gate over the Great Eau. Cross it and take the track to Saltfleet and turn right at the road. Cross Black Gowt Sluice bridge and turn right into Haven Bank.

3 Walk along the Haven as far as you wish but return to the car park and picnic site. Take the path behind the central picnic table through the dunes to the wide track on the perimeter of the saltmarsh. Wind along this trail and aim for the handrail in a clump of evergreen trees. Leave the saltmarsh by this ramp and go down Sea Lane, past the Sunnydale Holiday park. There is a small shop here. Turn left at the T junction and then right into Pump Lane. Pass the well-trimmed hedge and take the footpath to the right over a stile and small footbridge.

4 Cross the fields until you reach a waymarker, where you turn left down Louth Road. Pass Hill Top Farm and then continue on the path on the right. This path generally runs parallel to Mar Dyke but you will have to deviate slightly to cross the Grayfleet Drain and then resume your course to the B1200. Turn right at the road and, if you wish, stop for refreshments at the Old Church Gallery and Tea Rooms. From here go through the lych gate and churchyard, then cross two fields and stiles to the next road to turn left and return to Rimac.

FACT FILE

Distance 6 miles
Time 3 hours
Maps OS Landranger 113, OS Pathfinder TF 49
Start/parking Saltfleetby-Theddlethorpe Dunes entrance at Rimac car park, grid ref 467917
Terrain Good paths, some thorny shrubs in the sand dunes
Nearest town Mablethorpe
Refreshments The Old Church Gallery & Tea Rooms, Saltfleetby; the Prussian Queen pub, Saltfleetby; the Crown pub, Saltfleet
Public transport Daily service during school holidays only from Mablethorpe by Appleby's, tel 01507 358781
Stiles Few
Suitable for Children, dogs on leads in fields

ALONG THE WAY

It is an invigorating experience walking with a fresh sea breeze blowing through the sand dunes amid the wildlife that thrives there. Pleasure boats have now replaced the smugglers' vessels in Saltfleet Haven, where a variety of birds feed and children still play in the mud! It was mentioned in the Domesday book as one of the royal ports. In 1854 it was straightened when the natural course of the Great Eau was diverted to Saltfleet to scour the port of salt. This created a freshwater system in which a great variety of plants now grow, managed by annual cutting and burning.

Saltfleet • N

Saltfleet Haven

Hill Top Farm

Mar Dyke Drain

Great Eau

Sea View Farm

Start/ Finish

Saltfleet by St Clement

Rimac

Saltfleetby - Theddlethorpe Dunes Nature Reserve

VIEWS FROM THE CASTLE

Leave a busy port for the open horizons of Breydon Water and explore impressive Burgh Castle, the only disturbance being the call of curlews, oystercatchers and occasional burbling cruiser.

1 Set off north along the quay, crossing Haven Bridge to take the first turn right, Steam Mill Lane. At the corner, where there is a toilet and car park, keep straight ahead on the footpath, then on the street. Just past the netted play area go right on the footpath to the river, then left. Keep on the footpath over the flood wall and back, passing various boats, and finally go under the A47 bridge.

2 Follow the Breydon Water bank on the Angles Way for 3½ miles. This is a good track at the start then becomes a grassy path just behind the steel flood barrier. It eventually curves left to Church Farm. When funds are available the bank is to be heightened and a temporary diversion will be provided.

3 Cross the stile opposite the farm to a footpath sign. Turn right between reeds and rising ground, keeping straight ahead for ¼ mile to a T junction. Go left to leave the Angles Way. Near the end of the wall there are information boards. Continue east on this path and soon turn left to the church and club entrances. Go right along the road, keeping straight on for 1 mile, past the pub then some interesting houses. The road is narrow, so keep to the right.

4 At a bend and postbox turn off left and go right, straight past Crow's Farm. Take a slight dogleg to enter the field. Go through the next fence and straight ahead at a signed footpath. Go 5yds left at the next houses then right through a kissing gate, keeping straight round a barrier to reach Bradwell Hall. Go straight on past farm buildings to bear right to a track and chain link fencing.

5 Turn left towards Gapton Marshes, then go right on the worn path beside the industrial estate fencing. The path descends to cross the ditch and back again before reaching a road. Follow the verge left for 85yds, then turn right on a footpath between fences to reach another road. Go right and left down Boundary Road, veering left at the end where you cross a footbridge over the carriageways.

6 Head east over the road junction towards the river, then go left past the various shipping and dockyard installations to the Haven Bridge.

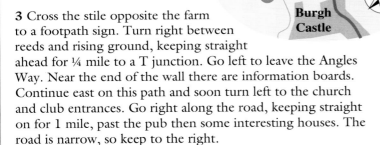
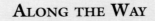

The ruins of Burgh Castle

ALONG THE WAY

The large thatched building near the bridge at the start was an ice house, the ice being stored for fish preservation in summer. The Angles Way starts near the station and connects with the Peddars and Icknield Ways. Burgh Castle, built in Norman times, is on the site of what was once a Roman fort. Three side walls remain with their added turrets, built of flint bonded with bricks. The castle gives a good view over the marshes and the old wind pumps, especially Berney Arms just opposite.

FACT FILE

Distance 9 miles
Time 5 hours
Maps OS Landranger 134, OS Pathfinder 904
Start/parking Free car park on east quayside south of Haven Bridge, beyond preserved *Lydia Eva* steam drifter, grid ref 523072
Terrain Flat and easy
Nearest town Great Yarmouth
Refreshments Church Farm Country Club, open to non-residents 11.30am–3pm, or Queens Head pub. Vast choice at start
Public transport Good rail and bus services
Stiles Several, some high but you can duck under
Suitable for Older children, dogs on leads

ON THE WING

Treat yourself to an excellent wood, old railway and sea bank walk, including an exceptional migratory bird reserve.

1 From the car park go north then west down Alma Road. Just past Cherry Tree Road go through the kissing gate at the farm entrance and follow the field path to trees and the bypass (cross carefully). Keep straight ahead into Ken Hill Wood. The path soon rises and levels out to lead to the westerly edge and a junction. Follow the left fence to pass behind Lodge Hill Farm, descending to an old track, and then turn right to the farm. Turn left at the barn on a good track that heads towards the sea. Go right then left to cross the old railway and on to field gates and a footpath sign.

2 Go through the first gate, keeping to the left side of the field, and over a stone-filled channel. Veer right across the field to another one, cross it and then the left bridge into the next field. Turn left and cross the field to a kissing gate and bridge – you may find a path circling left on drier ground. Go through the kissing gate and up the bank, veering left to reach a bird hide on the next sea bank.

3 Follow the bank left for 2 miles, perhaps stopping to read the RSPB information boards at the car park. If you prefer, you can walk on the sheltered chalet road, eventually returning to the bank.

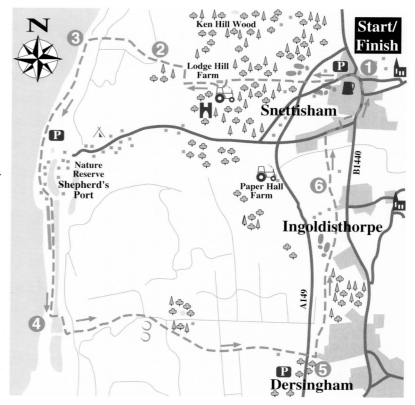

4 At the two benches and memorial seat take the footpath left, passing over a pits causeway, then right along its side for 327yds to a fence/stile. Turn left up over the bank, over a grassy strip and concrete bridge. Follow another strip to a concrete road, which you take west to the A149. Cross the road carefully and continue until you are opposite the old railway station.

5 Turn left on the old railway path to Ingoldisthorpe old gatehouse – there is no right of way ahead. Go 24yds right then left over two iron fences on a path beside the property. The right of way goes straight ahead to a track at the end of the field, bearing away from the railway. The worn path swings on to the old railway and follows it for 125yds. After that it veers right over the field to a track junction.

6 Continue ahead, going north-north-west on the worn path to pass a watermill on the right. You soon reach the beach road, where you turn right then left opposite St Mary's church hall. Go right along a rear entrance access. At the end go left along the road, then right down Southgate Lane to the main road. Here turn left again to return to the start.

FACT FILE

Distance 9 miles
Time 4½ hours
Maps OS Landranger 132, OS Pathfinder 839
Start Snettisham shops car park, grid ref 685342
Parking At start or Beach car park or picnic area on bypass, grid ref 679303
Terrain Almost flat, some banks and undulations in wood, water meadows can be wet

Nearest town Hunstanton
Refreshments Queen Victoria and Compasses pubs in Snettisham
Public transport On Hunstanton/ King's Lynn route 410 & 411
Stiles Four
Suitable for Fit children, dogs on leads

If you're interested in bird life allow yourself plenty of time and join the birdwatchers on the sea bank. At high tide the birds are driven inland off the mudflats, and some end up on the pits behind the bank. Snettisham beach, with its varied accommodation from proudly kept bungalows to run-down shacks, is always interesting and seldom crowded, even in high summer. The old railway was closed in 1969 after 107 years in operation, but is now a peaceful and sheltered path.

The tree-lined track at Ken Hill Wood, near the start of the walk

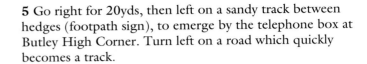

SEA AND SKY

Enjoy this walk on a clear, crisp day, with no sound but the birds and the sea.

1 From the church, walk north up the main street and follow the lane out of the village for nearly 2 miles. There is not much traffic but what there is moves fast; take care. A permissive forest track on the left cuts off the corner.

2 Turn left at the crossroads and just after a large red-brick house turn right on a bridleway. Keep left at a fork and emerge on a forest track. Follow this to the left and go straight ahead at a crossroads on a stony track which brings you to the Forest Office.

3 Go straight on along the tarmac road, pass through a gate and turn right. Just before the caravan site, go straight ahead through a camping area, and through a barrier at the far end to a sandy track parallel to the caravan site. Take the first track left (not shown on the map, but one of the Forestry Commission's waymarked cycle trails). At a T junction, go right on a stony track to the lane.

4 Cross to a sandy track straight ahead, bear right at a fork and emerge on the Butley road. Turn right. Near the end you can see Butley Priory on your right.

5 Go right for 20yds, then left on a sandy track between hedges (footpath sign), to emerge by the telephone box at Butley High Corner. Turn left on a road which quickly becomes a track.

6 Go right on a sandy track at the field corner, with Burrow Hill ahead. Follow the track through a waymarked gate and make the very short climb to the summit and a first view of the sea.

7 Bear right to a stile and follow a clear path downhill to a gate and stile. Go left on the track, cross another stile and climb the dyke.

8 Here the Butley Ferry will take you (and bicycles) across the Butley River to Orford, if you want a really long day out. For this route, though, turn right to begin a lovely airy walk of 3 miles on the top of the dyke. As you round Flybury Point, there is a good view back to Orford with its castle, and the lighthouse and mysterious pagoda-like buildings on Orford Ness. The marshes and rivers abound with water birds, and the shingle spit across the River Ore is all that separates you from the sea.

9 Just as you see the breakers crashing around the end of the spit, the dyke veers inland and turns sharp right up the river to the road bridge.

10 Climb the ladder stile and turn left to make your way back to Hollesley along the lanes.

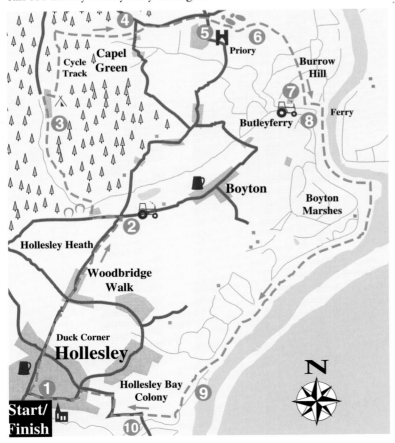

FACT FILE

Distance 11½ miles
Time 5–6 hours
Map OS Landranger 169
Start/parking Hollesley church, grid ref 354444
Terrain Easy, clear paths and tracks
Nearest town Woodbridge
Refreshments Two pubs in Hollesley
Public transport Information from County Connections, tel 01473 265676. There is a rowing boat ferry across the Butley River (grid ref 391482). Tel 01394 410096 to check times and availability
Stiles Lots
Suitable for Older children

The Suffolk coast is so tranquil today that it is hard to associate these empty marshes and heaths with military activity. Yet this coastline has always been open to invasion – first the Angles and Saxons and then the Vikings settled here uninvited. The Martello Towers were built to guard against Napoleon, and more recently still the concrete tank traps and gun emplacements bristling from lonely beaches and quiet lanes were intended to prevent a German invasion. Radar was developed a few miles away at RAF Bawdsey, Orford Ness was used for testing detonators, and it seemed every other field was an air base. Now all is peaceful again and birds, walkers and yachtsmen have the coast to themselves.

If you want to extend your day, take the Butley Ferry across to Orford at point 8

WINTER REFUGE

An ideal walk for birdwatchers, especially when the winter visitors arrive.

1 Take the driveway beside the cottage opposite the pub, following a footpath sign. At the field edge, take the right fork, a broad grassy path across meadows, with duckboards laid over the boggy area at the bottom. After a footbridge over a drainage channel, the boards end and the broad path continues along the field edge to the river.

2 Climb the dyke and turn left. Levington church looks very pretty on the bank behind you, and the forest of masts in the marina can be seen ahead. Follow the well-walked path along the dyke to the head of the little creek.

3 Cross an area of hard-standing (the gate on the left gives access to parking at the end of a lane from the village), and take a clear path by a lone tree to rejoin the dyke and follow it down the other side of the creek. The lake on your left (which is not marked on OS maps) is Levington Lagoon, recently created as a wetland habitat.

4 Keep right and follow the dyke on the river's edge, skirting the marina's silt pans on your left.

5 At the marina, turn left up through the boatyard and make your way along the top of the marina to the access road.

6 Just past the barrier, there is a sandy area on the right. A narrow path from the far right corner of this leads to a delightful path through woods above the river. At the end of the wood, bear right on the obvious path around the lake and follow the causeway between lake and river.

7 Go over the fence by the gate – the stile is missing but the fence is easy to climb and dogs can get between the rails. Once over it, turn left on a sandy track. Go round the next gate, then halfway to the buildings look out for a narrow but clear path down through the field on your left. At the bottom, join a track and bear right into the trees to a footpath sign at a path junction. Cross the stream and follow the path up the field.

8 Bear left on to the track by the cottage. Before reaching the level crossing, turn left on the drive to Morston Hall. Pass the Hall on your right and go through a gate in the far left corner of the yard – this leads you on to a grassy track between barns. Bear right on to a sandy track running between fields. This abruptly becomes a narrow but clear path descending sharply through the brackeny scrub of Fire Hill. It then starts to climb less sharply up the far side of the dip to join another field track.

9 At the concrete drive, turn right. When you reach the lane, turn left to return to Levington.

FACT FILE

Distance 5½ miles
Time 2–3 hours
Map OS Landranger 169
Start Ship Inn, Levington, grid ref 234390
Parking Levington village (with consideration), or alternative start at point 3
Terrain Easy, all clear paths
Nearest town Felixstowe
Refreshments Ship Inn, Levington
Public transport Information from County Connections, tel 01473 265676
Stiles One, broken but fence is easy to negotiate
Suitable for Children and dogs

ALONG THE WAY

The mudflats and lagoons on this route are home to many birds, including lapwings, oystercatchers, moorhens and swans, and provide temporary refuge to many more, including plovers, dunlin, shelduck, sandpipers and avocets. The views downriver are dominated by the cranes of Felixstowe Dock, and the return route by Morston Hall gives fine views to the much older port of Harwich and the tall clock tower on the old Customs House.

If you thought the name Levington sounded familiar, the chances are that you've seen it at your local garden centre. Levington composts, fertilisers and other garden products all take their name from this village, and the company's headquarters and research station are still here.

When you have finished the walk, you can return to the comfort of the Ship Inn in Levington

WALES

HOLY ISLAND

Allow plenty of time for this walk on Holyhead Mountain and enjoy the variety of sights along the way.

1 On the rough ground opposite the car park there is a group of well-preserved hut-circles (Cytiau'r Gwyddelod). Cross the stone stile at the entrance and walk up to the notice board. Further up and to the right an arrow on a post indicates a path to a second group of huts. Beyond these it narrows to a twisting line through the gorse and in 100yds you can fork left and clamber up to a track. Turn right and follow it to a cottage called Foel.

2 Where the track ends take the path going right. It is narrow at first, then more open as it crosses the hillside above a reservoir, making for the right flank of Holyhead Mountain. Climb to the ridge then go left up its rocky crest to the trig point on the summit.

3 Follow a path that descends eastwards, on the line of the large breakwater that forms Holyhead harbour. In about 200yds, pass through an old stone dyke which is part of Caer y Twr, the hillfort that once occupied the top of the hill. In a further 200yds you reach a path running at right angles. Turn left on a contouring line that comes alongside a power line then drops down quite steeply to the Fog Signal Station overlooking North Stack.

4 Return to the top of the final descent then turn right on a path that climbs up over the shoulder of the hill with sea cliffs on your right. Descend a section with steps then pass a radio repeater station before bearing right again, past a small lake, to a ruined pillbox. From there keep left and downhill to a road end.

5 An arch marks the start of the steps down to the lighthouse on South Stack. There are plans to develop a visitor's centre on the site but at present there is no access to the Stack. Despite this it is worth going down the steps for views of the cliffs – just remember that every step down means one back up again! Finally walk down the road then turn right by a café to reach the bird observatory at Ellen's Tower, from where a cliff top path leads back to the car park.

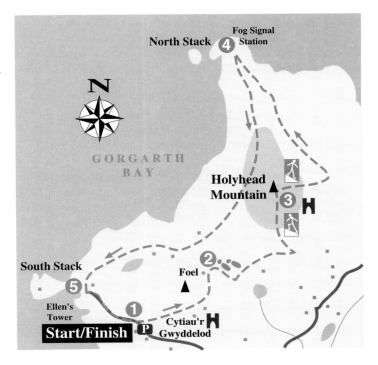

ALONG THE WAY

Holyhead Mountain dominates the north end of Ynys Gybi and the town of Holyhead. As you cross its summit you will come across fine prehistoric remains and enjoy superb views of the nearby coast. On clear days the peaks of Snowdonia range across the southern skyline and if you're very lucky you might see Ireland and the Isle of Man. The sea cliffs are popular with rock climbers but they also hold important seabird colonies and there is an RSPB observatory at Ellen's Tower near the end of the walk.

FACT FILE

Distance 4½ miles
Time 3–4 hours
Maps OS Landranger 114, OS Pathfinder 734
Start/parking RSPB car park on left of road, grid ref 211818
Terrain Rough paths and tracks, boots advised
Nearest town Holyhead
Refreshments Café (seasonal) near end of walk
Public transport Bus or train to Holyhead then Ynys Môn 22 to South Stack. Refer to Ynys Môn Public Transport Timetable
Stiles One
Suitable for Dogs and children but take care near cliff edges

South Stack lighthouse

COASTAL HERITAGE

Visit some historical landmarks on this trail through a country park.

1 From the Visitor Centre walk south-west between buildings and turn left on to the lane opposite the site of the Abbey Wire Mill. Pass the old Cotton Mill and fork right at the reservoir which once powered the machinery. A hundred yards beyond the reservoir fork left into woods, then keep right at the intersection ahead, now on a level track. Pass steps on the left signed 'Panoramic Walk' and in 50yds turn right down some steps past a square chimney to cross the Battery Pool dam. Turn left along a stony path rising to the B5121 road at the Royal Oak.

2 Cross the road and immediately fork left up Bryn Celyn Lane. Where its surface deteriorates by a large residence, turn off right at a footpath sign by a rusty post. Continue round the back of a housing estate to a gate and single-bar stile on the left. Cross over and walk along with the hedge with superb estuary views to your right. Pass through a hedge gap ahead and over the next field to cross an old gate in trees above Ty Coch Farm.

3 Walk across the following field and left along the rising edge of the next one, crossing a stile by an ash tree on the downhill side. Another field follows, then a grassy track past a farm. Cross the stile ahead and aim half-right downhill to cross a footbridge over a stream in the woods and then rise to meet a lane. Turn right and in 50yds go left over a stile, heading for a telegraph pole. The stile here leads into a descending field path and at the bottom you take a line linking three oak trees to reach a track in a copse by the A548 coast road.

4 Cross the road and walk left along the pavement. Just past Yr Hen Dafarn pub and the market, a footpath heads for the estuary shore with a stream on your left. Pass under the railway and approach the *Duke of Lancaster* liner, which is a splendid sight at close quarters.

5 Bear right and walk along the shore behind boulder flood defences. Further on there is an alternative embankment path 20yds inland.

6 In 1½ miles you reach a gate and a road alongside the once thriving but now sadly neglected Greenfield Dock. The road leads over the railway to the A548. Turn left and take a footpath from the far corner of the Heritage Valley car park, passing the ruins of Basingwerk Abbey and returning to the Visitor Centre.

FACT FILE

Distance 5 miles
Time 3 hours
Map OS Landranger 116
Start/parking Greenfield Valley Heritage Park Visitor Centre, grid ref 195775
Terrain Good tracks, field paths and estuary embankment
Nearest Town Holywell
Refreshments Royal Oak pub near start, Yr Hen Dafarn pub at Dee estuary
Public transport Crosville Coastliner No XI bus between Llandudno and Chester
Stiles Several, a few of which are awkward – difficult for dogs
Suitable for Older children

ALONG THE WAY

The Greenfield Valley Heritage Park is 12 miles of woodlands, reservoirs, ancient monuments and industrial history. At the start are Basingwerk Abbey ruins, the Abbey Farm Museum and a Visitor Centre. Reaching the Dee estuary shoreline you pass close to the *Duke of Lancaster* – this beached liner is a well-known local landmark.

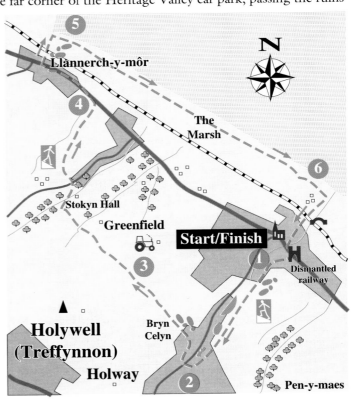

The beached Duke of Lancaster liner can be seen at close quarters as you approach point 5

LOVER'S ISLAND

Ynys Llanddwyn, off Anglesey, is a fascinating place to visit at any time of the year. It is particularly appropriate to go there in the spring for it takes its name from the church of St Dwynwen, who in Wales is the patron saint of those in love.

1 The lane leading to the car park continues as a green path with nature reserve enclosures on the left. It leads past a stone ruin called Cwt-gwlyb to the corner of a forest. You then walk for a straight mile along the edge of the forest until you reach the shore of Llanddwyn Bay, where there are fine views across the water to the hills of the Lleyn Peninsula.

2 Ynys Llanddwyn is away to the right – walk in that direction on the shore of a wide curving beach. Rocky outcrops mark Gwddw Llanddwyn, where a sandy spit connects the island to the mainland (gwddw is Welsh for neck). Cross here, go up some steps on the right and then follow a path along the spine of the island, past the ruins of a church, to the old lighthouse and pilots' cottages at the end.

3 Make your way back to the neck and so to the mainland. Turn right, back along the beach for 300yds to a track that goes up through the dunes then curves right through trees to a clearing.

4 Turn left on a forest track, then in 200yds go straight on past a boulder. This track runs in a north-easterly direction and you should keep with it to a crossroads at a clear section where the trees have been felled. A green ride continues in the same direction to an iron gate at the edge of the forest. From here a track leads on over rough ground and soon bears right to a road.

5 Turn left, then at a T junction by a cemetery turn right down a lane that leads to your outward path at a nature reserve sign. Turn left and you will soon be back at the start.

FACT FILE

Distance 7 miles
Time 3 hours, but allow extra time to explore the island
Maps OS Landranger 114, OS Pathfinder 768
Start/parking Small car park 400yds down the lane that runs south-west from the roundabout on the A4080 at Pen-lan, grid ref 426647
Terrain Sandy paths, beach, forest tracks
Nearest town Llangefni
Refreshments None on the walk
Public transport Ynys Môn 42 from Llangefni or Bangor
Stiles None
Suitable for Children, also dogs but please observe nature reserve signs

ALONG THE WAY

Ynys Llanddwyn is a National Nature Reserve, and there are several informative notice boards along the walk. Look out for the Soay sheep which may be in grazing plots in the dunes or on the island. Near the start is a hide from which wildfowl on Llyn Rhos-ddu can be observed.

The old lighthouse on Ynys Llanddwyn

CASTLES AND COAST

The stretch of coast to the west of Caernarfon is a popular walk for local people.
Here we extend it to the wide shores of Foryd Bay then return by an inland route
with views to the mountains of Snowdonia.

1 From the quayside by the castle a swing bridge (Bont yr Aber) leads to the far shore. Cross, turn right and follow a quiet coastal road beside the Menai Straits. After about 1½ miles the shore swings south into Foryd Bay – look out for an isolated church by a few trees on the left.

2 A gate and sign indicate the start of a path across a field to the walls of Llanfaglan churchyard. It continues in the same line to a ladder stile then beside a hedge to a gate. In the far corner of the next field it goes through an iron gate into Tan-y-graig farmyard.

3 Cross the yard and follow the farm track to a road. Turn left and go uphill past a chapel, 250yds beyond which you turn right through a gate. Follow a track that curves left through some old farm buildings to a gate. Bear left uphill to a small gate and footpath sign where you turn right and cross a field to a white house. Turn right and follow the approach track down to the road.

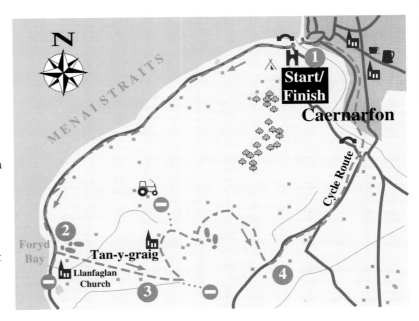

4 Turn left and in ¼ mile after crossing a bridge, drop onto a cycleway and footpath on the left. Go right on this old railway line, back into Caernarfon. The path emerges close to the wharf car park and the castle.

FACT FILE

Distance 6½ miles
Time 3 hours
Maps OS Landranger 115, OS Pathfinder 768
Start/parking On the quay by Caernarfon castle, grid ref 478626
Terrain Coastal road, then field paths and tracks – wet in places
Nearest town Caernarfon
Refreshments There is a wide choice of cafés and pubs in Caernarfon
Public transport Caernarfon is well served by buses. Copies of the Gwynedd Transport Guide can be obtained from tourist information offices
Stiles One
Suitable for Children and dogs. The coastal section is suitable for wheelchair users

ALONG THE WAY

Foryd Bay is a good habitat for shore birds. Curlews, oystercatchers and redshanks are among those you can expect to see. The old churchyard of Llanfaglan, where the main part of the church building dates from the 13th century, is a peaceful place to take a break.

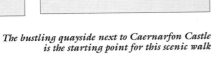

The bustling quayside next to Caernarfon Castle is the starting point for this scenic walk

COASTAL HERITAGE

The Lleyn Heritage Coast is one of the best-kept secrets in Wales. For tranquillity go there in winter and enjoy an unspoilt area at its best.

1 Head away from the village for a short distance, then turn right into a lane (signed to beach). In 100yds take a footpath across fields on the left. At the third ladder stile aim to the right of buildings to another stile that leads you on to a track. Turn right and follow it down to a minor road.

2 Turn left and follow this very quiet road for just over 2 miles to the crossroads at Pen-y-graig. Over the hedges there are views of the sea to your right.

3 Turn right and head up past a chapel and shop, then go straight on down a lane to the sea at Porth Colmon.

4 On the right, steps lead up to a gate and the cliff top path which takes you to the wide expanse of Traeth Penllech. Here firm sands give easy walking, unless the tide forces you on to the path before you reach the end of the beach. Eventually you will have to climb the steep bank and regain the cliff top path before, ¼ mile further on, you drop down to the pebbly beach in Porth Ychain.

5 Beyond, a path leads back to the top of the cliff and takes you to National Trust land, where the little bay called Porth Gwylan would make a sheltered lunch spot. The next bay is Porth Ysgaden, where coal yards, evidence of the former coastal trade, can still be seen. The coast now swings right and care is needed on a short section of eroded path.

6 Porth Towyn is identified by another sandy bay. Here you turn right after passing a small caravan site to reach a road. Cross this and pass through the yard of Towyn Farm. You then follow a gated track up to Tudweiliog, where you turn right on the B4417 to return to the start.

ALONG THE WAY

Once you reach Porth Colmon you embark on an uninhabited stretch of coast with a wide sandy bay, rocky headlands and small coves. Look for oystercatchers and ringed plovers on the sands and turnstones foraging among the rocks; you might also be lucky enough to see the rare chough, the bird that is the symbol of the Heritage Coast.

FACT FILE

Distance 9½ miles
Time 4–5 hours
Maps OS Landranger 123, OS Pathfinder 821
Start/parking Layby on the B4414 south of Tudweiliog, grid ref 232363
Terrain Quiet roads, coast path and beach, can be muddy in places
Nearest town Pwllheli
Refreshments Pub in Tudweiliog
Public transport Bws Gwynedd no 8 from Pwllheli to Tudweiliog
Stiles Numerous
Suitable for Children, dogs on leads in places

Impressive sea stacks at the north end of Traeth Penllech

WHERE THE SAND WHISTLES

An unspoilt coastline is something to treasure, so it is good to know that most of the stretch followed on this walk is in the safe hands of the National Trust.

1 From the car park walk down to the beach at Porth Oer, also known as Whistling Sands because of the way the sand squeaks when you walk on it. Clamber up rocks on the left and follow a narrow path round a headland. Almost at once there is a zigzag path, signposted to Anelog, which leads up to the top of the cliff. Walk up this, then enjoy easy walking beside a fence with steep grass slopes on your right. Alternatively, take a more adventurous line just above the rocks. Both lines meet at a kissing gate about ¾ mile from Porth Oer and a path continues along the cliff top until you can descend to a footbridge at Porthorion.

2 Cross the stile and go up a steep grass slope to a fence, bear right and follow it to an old stile. Continue the climb until you reach another stile at the next fence, then make your way up tracks that wind through gorse and heather. After a short descent head towards the isolated white-washed cottage called Mount Pleasant.

3 A clear path bears left behind the cottage, but you soon leave this to make the short climb to the top of Mynydd Anelog (628ft). There are outstanding views, not only of the surrounding coast and out to the lighthouse on Bardsey Island, but also in clear weather the whole sweep of Wales from Anglesey, by way of Snowdonia, down the coast to Pembrokeshire. With luck you may also see Ireland far out in the west. When you are ready to leave, descend eastwards to a small cottage flanked by two iron roofs.

4 Go down beside an earth bank left of the cottage for 100yds, then turn left and follow a clear path that curves down to an iron gate behind a farmhouse. A track then leads down to a narrow road. Turn left and follow its winding course to the junction at Capel Carmel.

5 Turn left, then just short of the farm buildings at Carreg take a left turn to a National Trust car park. Go through the gate at the top, turn right and go through a second gate before climbing up to the round lookout at the top of Mynydd Carreg. This is another good viewpoint from which you can look back over the area you have walked. Walk down towards the sea, then turn right on the track that contours the base of the hill to arrive back at the road. Turn left and in 200yds go left again to return to the start.

ALONG THE WAY

Ravens and wintering flocks of curlew are a feature of this coast. You may also see the rare chough, which has been adopted as the symbol of the Lleyn Heritage Coast. Seals are often seen offshore – but don't be confused by buoys marking lobster pots.

The rocky shoreline to the west of Porth Oer

FACT FILE

Distance 6 miles
Time 3 hours
Maps OS Landranger 123, OS Pathfinder 843
Start/parking National Trust car park at Porth Oer, grid ref 166295
Terrain Firm paths and quiet lanes
Nearest town Pwllheli
Refreshments In the holiday season enjoy an excellent tea at Carreg Plas, grid ref 164290
Public Transport In summer a Walkers' Bus (Bws Llyn) passes Porth Oer twice daily
Stiles Two
Suitable for Children, dogs on leads due to grazing sheep

COASTAL INSPIRATION

Magnificent coastal scenery makes this an inspiring walk, with the sheltered beach at Llangranog inviting you to rest a while. Look out for dolphins!

1 Go left, passing the Cartws Café (seasonal) on your left. Go through a gate to cross the lane and turn right with a signposted track towards Llangranog. Fork left at the foot of a hill and climb with a track which overlooks the bay and beach on your left.

2 Don't go through the gate but fork left over a stile and walk along the waymarked cliff top path with the sea on your left. Pass a radio mast on your right and follow the waymarked path downhill. Turn right down steps, cross a stile and a stream in the bottom of a valley and climb the other side, keeping to the left-hand edge of a field.

3 Reach a road at a hairpin bend and fork left down into Llangranog. Walk to the northern end of the beach and go up a flight of steps. Follow the coastal path, with the sea on your left, to the peninsula opposite Ynys-Lochtyn.

4 Retrace your steps uphill with the sea now on your right. Turn left along a track and soon afterwards bear right through bracken to reach an access lane which you follow down towards Llangranog.

5 Turn right to take the road towards the beach. Go left to walk with the sea on your right, back uphill to the hairpin bend. Go inland this time with the road which climbs to pass Maes-y-morfa and the buildings of Morfa-uchaf on your left. Pass a road on your left, then the access lane to Morfa Canol on your right. Don't be tempted by a hedged track on your right when the road bends left. Go ahead a few yards to the next hedged track on your right.

6 Turn right along the old green lane. Go ahead through a gate and pass woodland to reach a signposted path junction. Fork left downhill along your outward path back to the car park.

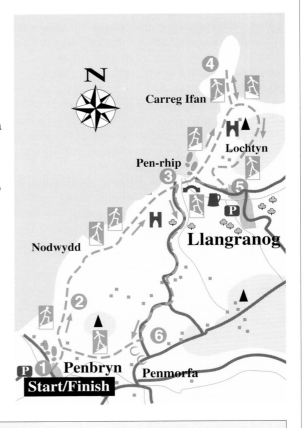

Superb coastal scenery near point 2

FACT FILE

Distance 9 miles
Time 5 hours
Maps OS Landranger 145, OS Pathfinder 988
Start/parking Penbryn car park, grid ref 296522
Terrain Cliff tops, with some steep ascents and descents, lanes inland
Nearest towns Cardigan or New Quay
Refreshments Llangranog, Cartws

Café, near start, in summer
Public transport None
Stiles Seven
Suitable for All

ALONG THE WAY

Tourists flock to the beaches at Llangranog and Penbryn today, but in the 6th century the traffic came in the other direction. As you climb with the track near the start of this walk and overlook the bay, imagine King Arthur's fleet down below and perhaps a battle being fought on the beach. There is a strong local tradition that the Battle of Llongborth was fought here, near Penbryn. Geraint, one of Arthur's knights, was killed in the battle and his grave is reckoned to be in this parish. It's certainly a special spot.

A DIFFERENT ANGLE

Walk through a history of coastal defences on this journey in an undiscovered corner of Pembrokeshire.

1 From the centre of Angle head east past the church and take the track just beyond to the left. This puts you on the Pembrokeshire Coast Path.

2 Follow the path as it hugs the foreshore around past the Old Point House pub, a 15th-century building with superb views, round Angle Point above the ruins of the Old Lifeboat Station.

3 Go across the access road to the new lifeboat station and up alongside the fields of North Hill where the pattern of medieval strip fields can be made out.

4 All along this next section of the walk you come across the massive remains of old fortifications that once dominated Milford Haven, but are now sinking into obscurity in the trees and undergrowth.

5 Rounding the point you look down on Thorn Island, once a Victorian fort – now a hotel – that makes an impressive looking deterrent to invasion. The path drops down from here to West Angle Bay by the ruins of some lime kilns before crossing to climb again on well waymarked paths across MOD land and past an ancient burial ground. Leaving the MOD land, the views across the Haven are of St Anne's Head with its dominant lighthouse, and the site of Henry Tudor's landing in 1485, on his way to win a kingdom at Bosworth Field.

6 The walking from Rat Island past Sheep Island to Guttle Hole is fairly easy with superb views, but once past this point the going becomes strenuous with steep climbs and descents to streams. The path is well marked and has several realignments, so follow the obvious waymarks.

7 Note the Iron Age fort remains between East and West Pickard Bay.

8 Descending to Gravel Bay, the path becomes easier, and there are superb views to Castle Martin Ranges. At low tide you can see the remains of an ancient drowned forest in the bay, while the expanse of golden sands has few visitors.

9 From the west end of the bay pick up a little-used, waymarked footpath. This takes you inland across a field into a boggy stream valley, across the middle of a second field, to a gate into a third field. Follow the left-hand hedge up to a gate on to the road.

10 Turn left and then follow the road for about 350yds until you reach a junction. Turn right down this quiet lane,

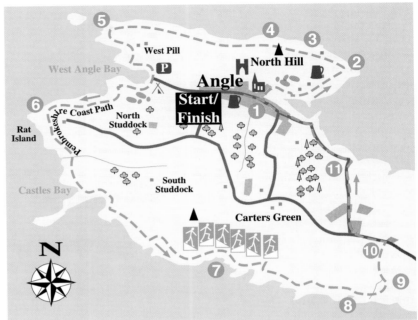

bordered by woods, and follow to the foreshore of the Haven.

11 Turn left to reach a quiet, private, foreshore road which leads you back to Angle.

FACT FILE

Distance 9½ miles
Time 5 hours
Maps OS Landranger 157, OS Pathfinder 1103, OS Outdoor Leisure 36
Start Centre of Angle, grid ref 864029
Terrain Mainly good coast paths, some steep ascents and descents.
Nearest town Pembroke Parking at start by Hibernia Inn or at West Angle Bay, grid ref 853031
Refreshments Café, West Angle Bay and Hibernia Inn, Angle
Public transport Limited service to Angle from Pembroke
Stiles Thirty-seven
Suitable for Dogs on leads over farmland and where signed. Keep children under control on cliff paths

ALONG THE WAY

The importance of this remote corner of the Pembrokeshire National Park is shown by the fortifications found along this walk. The waterway of Milford Haven, now dominated by oil refineries and power stations, which do not intrude on this walk, has been guarded from earliest times. Remains of Iron Age, Victorian and more recent defences are passed along the way.

BURIALS AND INVASIONS

In only 5 miles, this walk takes in both striking coastal scenery and a surprising number of sites of historical interest, including a neolithic cemetery and the site of the last French invasion of mainland Britain.

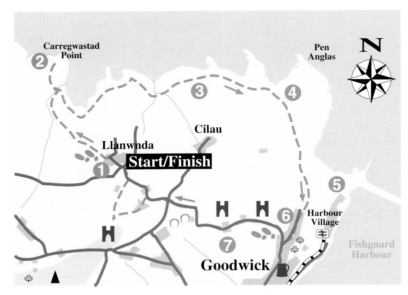

1 The walk starts from the centre of Llanwnda, a quiet and attractive hamlet, worth a few minutes' investigation in its own right. The church, restored in 1870, is of an ancient Celtic bellcote type and the boulder-strewn green was once the site of a stone circle, showing this place to have been important for religious ceremonies long before Christianity. From the green, cross the stile with a fingerpost pointing to 'Carregwastad Footpath' on to National Trust land, where you follow a sometimes muddy path past an ancient 'holy' well and alongside a magnificently restored house with a traditional Pembrokeshire cement-washed roof. Follow the fingerpost signs on to a broad track down to a stile and gate into a field, then along the right-hand hedge and into a green lane. At the end of the lane go straight across a field to a gateway into a further field where you follow the right-hand boundary to the corner, then cut diagonally across the field to a fingerpost and gate on to the coastal path.

2 To visit Carregwastad Point with its memorial stone to the French Invasion, turn left and down into the charming wooded dingle of Cwm Felin, which is alive with birdsong and the sound of the stream that may well have driven Llanwnda's mill, before climbing up to gain the headland. It was here, on 22 February 1797, that 1,500 French soldiers landed, intent on marching through Wales and raising the Principality against the Crown. After admiring the view from this historic spot, retrace your route across Cwm Felin and follow the coastal path past the field gate and along the undulating cliffs above craggy coves.

3 The route from here to Harbour Village follows the obvious coast path with superb views, especially from the high point of Carnfathach, one of the many volcanic outcrops in the area.

4 From Anglas Bay the route bears more inland on good paths and green lanes. As the path curves southward you pass some ruined cottages and traces of wartime defences in the form of ruinous concrete, erected to protect the harbour below.

5 Fishguard harbour was planned as a great transatlantic port, and from 1900 the cliffs were blasted and breakwaters built along with a rail terminus, passenger station, hotel, storage sheds, slipways and all the ancillary work such a port would entail. The path takes you from the open cliff top into Harbour Village, a settlement of unpretentious houses built in 1900 to accommodate the builders of the port below. Just beyond the telephone box, leave the coast path in favour of a narrow road on the right leading to Pen Rhiw.

6 At this point you can divert from the main route to investigate Garn Wen neolithic cemetery. Turn right into the car parking area behind the houses. At the far end follow the footpath to find three cromlechs aligned with the fence posts some 10yds from the garden wall. The cromlechs have massive cap stones resting partly on side stones and partly on the ground. At one time there may have been up to nine cromlechs here.

7 Retrace your steps to the track up to Pen Rhiw which improves to become a well-tarmacked drive. Just before reaching a bungalow (Ty Cromlech), you will find a plaque set into the bank on your left commemorating the first successful flight to Ireland from the adjacent field by Denys Corbet Wilson on 22 April 1912. Continue along the lane and just before entering Pen Rhiw farmyard note the superb cromlech standing tall in the field to your right. Pass straight through the farmyard and on along a green lane that curves under the rocky outcrop on your right and a small pond before bearing left. At a T junction of tracks, turn right and pass a riding stables before the track leads down to meet the road at a junction. Go straight on down the road signed Llanwnda past a large cemetery, then take the dead-end road to your left, signposted Public Footpath. This track winds up past a couple of houses and, following clear waymarks, climbs up through the grounds and outbuildings of another on to the rocky outcrop of Garnwnda. To visit yet another cromlech, take a faint path to your right just before the main path starts descending above a Bronze Age standing stone in a field to your left. Follow this path along the rocky crest of Garnwnda for some 100yds before taking an even fainter path that drops to the left, seemingly towards the white bungalow below. This will lead you to the well-preserved burial chamber that

has a commanding view over Llanwnda and the coastline. Retrace your steps to the path junction above the standing stone and turn right. At the next path junction turn right again and follow the path down to join the road to Llanwnda. Turn left on the road and you will soon be back at the centre of the hamlet and the start of the walk.

FACT FILE

Distance 5 miles
Time 3 hours
Maps OS Landranger 157, OS Pathfinder 1032, OS Outdoor Leisure 35
Start/parking Roadside parking in centre of Llanwnda, grid ref 932 395
Terrain Field paths, green lanes and coastal path
Nearest town Fishguard
Refreshments None
Public transport None
Stiles Fourteen or sixteen
Suitable for Children and dogs on leads

ALONG THE WAY

The French invasion commemorated in the memorial on Carregwastad Point lasted only 2 days. The soldiers got roaring drunk, met unexpected resistance in the Pembroke Militia, and finally mistook the red shawls and black bonnets of the local ladies for a reinforcing Redcoat regiment!

Despite the great plans for Fishguard, the First World War, combined with silting problems, meant that it never became a rival to Liverpool.

Enjoy superb views of the craggy coastline near Llanwnda

IN THE FOOTSTEPS OF THE WELSH SAINTS

Start from the tiny city of St Davids to enjoy a beautiful walk with ancient holy sites along the way.

1 From the car park walk west into the town to look down on the cathedral in its valley – sited here, it is said, either to avoid the attention of sea rovers, or because the swampy valley was the only place the local chieftain would allow the Christians land to build on – before taking the road west from the cross towards Porth Clais. Take the first turn to the left, then left again, then first right and up to a path that leads right behind the houses.

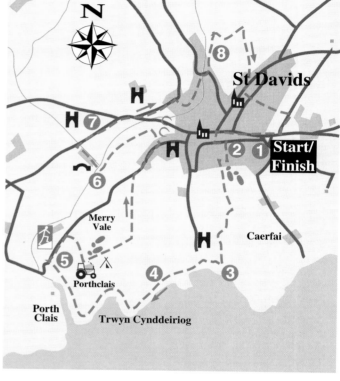

2 After about 100 yards, turn left on a path called Aarons Road, which leads a zigzag route down through fields to join the coast path by the modern monastery in St Nons Bay.

3 Turn right, then immediately right again off the coast path along a path under the monastery to St Nons Well and chapel in a field. Not much remains of the chapel, though there are low ruined walls and an interesting carved stone. The well, however, is still in working condition and the water tastes sweet. From the chapel, cross the wall by a stile in the far left of the field and rejoin the coastal path.

4 Follow this above cliffs frequented by birds and rock climbers until you reach Porth Clais, a narrow and beautiful harbour, with well-preserved lime kilns and an interesting footbridge (which you do not cross).

5 Turn right up the road and after some 300 yards turn right up a farm drive to Porthclais Farm. Just before entering the farmyard, turn left and, keeping the field boundary on your right, follow the path across two fields and into a green lane. Leave this lane immediately by an awkward stile on your left and follow the path down on to Waun Isaf Moor, where duckboards cover the boggiest sections of path, and down on to the road. Turn right and follow the road for approximately 300 yards to a green lane, Ffordd Melin Isaf (Little Mill Road), which drops left into Merry Vale, the valley of the River Alun. Swinging left, this path brings you down to a mill leat and eventually to an old mill.

6 Go through the gate and cross the garden of the mill to the driveway, which brings you out on to the road.

7 Turn right past the site of Parc y Castell, (which is variously described as the first settlement at St Davids, or a Norman Castle), to the road junction. Turn right, then left along a quiet road that gives good views of the cathedral, the close and the ruined palace. After 350 yards drop right down a rough lane beside the Palace to the Cathedral Close. Take the first turn left and follow this to Pont y Penyd Bridge, where pilgrims would wash their feet before entering St Davids.

8 Cross the bridge then turn left up the Pilgrim Route called Meidr Dwyll. Follow this as it climbs, swinging right after 300 yards, to a T junction of hedged paths. Turn right and follow the path as it zigzags its way back to St Davids via a small moor and a narrow lane on to Nun Street. On reaching the road, turn right, then after 50 yards turn left and up a back lane to New Street. Cross over and continue up the lane, which becomes a hedged path, past some houses. At the end of the path turn right on a quiet lane to the A487. Turn right, then immediately left, to arrive back at the start of the walk.

Distance 6 miles
Time 3 hours
Maps OS Landranger 157, OS Pathfinder 1055, OS Outdoor Leisure 35
Start/parking Grove car park grid ref 756252
Terrain Coast and field paths, muddy in places, and quiet lanes
Nearest Town St Davids
Refreshments Many cafés, pubs and hotels in St Davids
Public transport Regular buses from Haverfordwest (no 340) and Fishguard (no 411), weekdays only
Stiles Thirteen
Suitable for Children and dogs on leads

ALONG THE WAY

St Davids is Britain's smallest city and indeed is smaller than some villages. Founded in 1181 on the site of previous buildings, the cathedral, which is also on a reduced scale, is well worth a visit, as is the ruined Bishop's Palace, once the most splendid in the country. At one time an important site of pilgrimage, St Davids is quiet and peaceful, especially out of season. Porth Clais, an attractive harbour, features in Welsh and Arthurian legend, while St David himself is reputed to have been born to St Non during a thunderstorm at the chapel named for her, the healing well nearby springing up at the same instant.

The delightful harbour at Porth Clais

CLIFFS, BIRDS AND BEACHES

This walk not only offers tremendous cliff top views but also takes you to one of the best beaches in Pembrokeshire.

1 There are two possible starts to this walk. If the Ranges are not in use (ask in the village or look for the red flags on the Range) walk up through the village southwards on the road to St Govan's Head. At the car park at the end of the road, go on and down narrow and reputably uncountable steps to visit the chapel.

2 Regain the cliffs and follow the waymarked path past bunkers down to Broadhaven Sands. Cross the beach and join the path that follows the cliffs the other side.

1a Alternatively, if the Ranges are in use, leave the car park by the grassy path along its south side, past an interpretation board and down steps to the lily ponds.

2a Turn right and follow the path right to Broadhaven along the west side of the ponds, and then, taking the path on the left side of the bay, join the route following the cliffs.

3 This path leads along impressive cliffs which are riddled with caves and sink holes and important nesting sites for many species of birds. Follow the path around Stackpole Head and descend through a small wood to Barafundle Beach.

4 This is probably the best beach in Pembrokeshire and it is normally quiet (visitors have a fair walk to reach it from either direction). It is worth lingering here before climbing back up on to the cliffs through a deer park wall, and continuing on to Stackpole Quay. Built to import coal and export limestone, it was once the smallest harbour in Britain. Before climbing up the steps to join the road a visit to the National Trust tea rooms is recommended.

5 Once gained, the road leads past an unusual square lime kiln and National Trust holiday cottages and up to a road junction where you turn left and descend through Stackpole. Approximately 200yds after a 90° bend in the road and down a steep hill, turn left on to a grassy ride into the trees. Follow this for approximately 300yds before turning right on a boardwalk path which comes out at a T junction of paths after another 10yds.

6 You may wish to detour to see an interesting grotto to the right before following the path left and crossing Hidden Bridge,where you will appear to be walking on water to

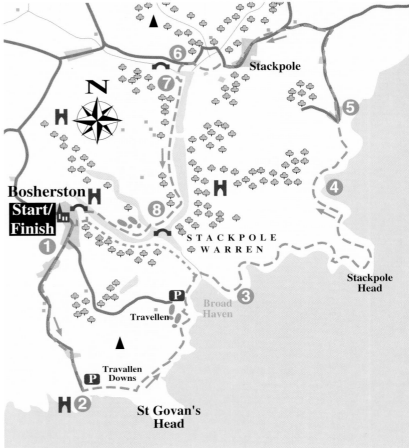

anyone standing on One Arch Bridge to your right. Climb up to the site of the former Stackpole Court. A short visit to the Old Game Pantry with its information display and history of the house is worthwhile.

7 From the terrace drop down noble steps and through an arch to join a path past the Old Boat House, now a wheelchair-accessible bird hide, and down past the attractive Eight Arch Bridge and along the lakeshore to Green Bridge.

8 Do not cross the bridge but go straight on for 200yds to a path junction. Where you drop left, cross one arm of the ponds on a causeway bridge and continue, under the banks of an Iron Age fort, to a second causeway bridge. This brings you to a track junction where you turn right to regain the start at the car park.

Distance 9 or 7 miles
Time 5 hours
Maps OS Landranger 158, OS Outdoor Leisure 36, OS Pathfinder 1124
Start/parking Bosherston car park, grid ref 966948
Terrain Cliff, lakeshore and woodland paths and quiet lanes
Nearest Town Pembroke
Refreshments National Trust tea rooms at Stackpole Quay; Armstrong Arms, Stackpole; Olde Worlde Café, St Govan's Inn, Bosherston
Public Transport None
Stiles Six
Suitable for Children and dogs on leads

ALONG THE WAY

The majority of this walk is on the Stackpole Estate, owned by the National Trust, and information panels are provided to help you enjoy the area.
If the MOD Ranges are not in use, the section around St Govan's Chapel is well worth walking, and a visit to the small 11th- or 13th-century chapel with its legendary links with St Govan and King Arthur is recommended. It stands on the site of a 5th-century hermit's cell.

The Bosherston lily ponds – limestone valleys that were flooded in the 18th century – form the largest area of fresh water in Pembrokeshire. Although they are famous for the lilies, which are best seen in June, these ponds are attractive all year round.

Barafundle Beach, one of the best in Pembrokeshire, is reached at point 4

SAND AND CASTLES

Enjoy a fascinating walk in an area rich in wildlife and visit two ruined castles.

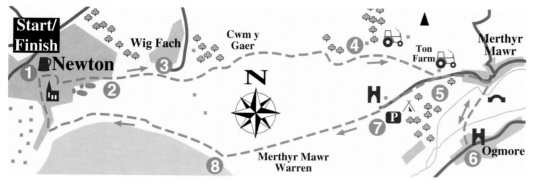

1 From the village green follow Church Road with the church on the right and the Jolly Sailor pub on the left. The road bends right and at the end of the allotments turn left on a track. Cross two roads, passing houses on the right. The track becomes a path which goes between bushes.

2 When you come out of the bushes the path turns right, but you keep ahead on another path. In about 60yds turn left on a narrower path. Follow it until you see a large house and its gardens directly behind a fence on the left. (This path turns left at the end of the garden.)

3 Opposite the house turn right, descending on a clear path. It becomes wider and reaches a flat grassy area. On the left look for two narrow paths rather close together. Take the second one and in 25yds take a narrower path left. The path becomes sandy and in 80yds reaches a fork. Take the right-hand one beside a low post with a yellow arrow. The path winds through the valley of Cwm y Gaer with its shrubs and coppiced trees. When it comes out in the open keep ahead on the waymarked path. Ignore a left-hand path at the next clump of trees. In another ½ mile you come to a farm gate beside a stone with waymarks. Continue through dense bushes and trees and descend through sand to a track.

4 Turn left and in about 50yds the track goes through some gateposts. Bear right to have a wall nearby on your right and reach a stone stile. Cross the stile and slant half-left uphill through the field. From the top of the hill head downhill with a wall and trees on your left to a stone stile. Continue with a fence on the left to another stile and a lane.

5 Bear left, passing St Teilo's church in Merthyr Mawr village. Opposite a lovely thatched cottage bear right on a track to a footbridge over the Ogmore River. Keep ahead to reach stepping stones across the Ewenni River and Ogmore Castle.

6 After looking around the castle ruins, return to the cottages of Merthyr Mawr. Turn left on the lane and follow it to its end at Candleston Castle.

7 Enter the car park and head south-south-west to a large sandy area. Keep a line of bushes on your right and go uphill to a gap between the bushes on the right and trees on the left. From the top of this hill go downhill, heading south-west, on a clear path to the left of a high sand dune. Continue on paths south-west or west that wind through buckthorn thickets and dunes and eventually reach the beach. On your left you can see Ogmore-by-Sea on its headland. On the right is Newton Point.

8 Follow the beach or the track above it to the car park near the houses at Newton. Turn right to follow the road to the village green.

FACT FILE

Distance 8½ miles
Time 4½ hours
Map OS Landranger 170
Start Newton village green, grid ref 835775
Parking Near the beach, not far from the village green
Terrain Easy walking on sand and grass paths

Nearest town Porthcawl
Refreshments Two pubs close to the start. Farm Teas near Ogmore Castle, also a pub nearby
Public transport Newton Village Green is on the route of some Porthcawl–Bridgend buses
Stiles A few, but easy
Suitable for Older children and dogs

Pass this sand dune at point 7 of the walk

ALONG THE WAY

Merthyr Mawr Warren is part of the Glamorgan Heritage Coast. Backed by a 200ft escarpment, the 600 acres of sand dunes are the second highest in Europe. This special habitat makes for interesting flora and fauna all year round. In spring and summer the many varieties of flowers and butterflies are a delight; look out for orchids and evening primrose. Autumn brings fungi and berries, fieldfare and redwing. In winter parts of the dunes may flood, attracting wildfowl.

Ogmore Castle is the shell of a Norman stronghold. Candleston Castle, also in ruins, was a fortified manor house.

SHAPED BY THE SEA

Amazing patterns on the beach and local legends make this an exciting walk.

1 From the bus stop opposite the Farmer's Arms, cross the grass towards Little Wood Cottage and pass it on your left. Go over the stone stile marked Seamouth and bear left. Halfway along the field cross another stile and follow the yellow arrows and stiles through the fields and a wood. Keep ahead past the Heritage Centre to Dunraven Bay.

2 Cross the stile into Dunraven Park. Take the main track to the walled gardens. A path through the gardens rejoins the track. Bear right to an information panel above the beach. If the tide is out, this is a fine viewpoint of the wave-cut platforms. The track continues to the site of Dunraven Castle and other paths on the left lead to Witch's Point and down to the beach. After your explorations return to the information panel to continue the walk.

3 Follow the cliff edge on your right and leave the track to walk beside a low fence. The path rises to a stile and continues on the cliffs before swinging left beside a wall. Descend through the thickets of Cwm Mawr to a plank bridge across a stream. The path climbs steeply to a ladder stile on the cliff top. Continue to another stile above the next valley, Cwm Bach.

4 Take a path slanting down into Cwm Bach and head up the valley, away from the coast, to a stile. Continue ahead, keeping by the left boundary in the third field, to an enclosed track and road. Turn left and immediately right on a narrow lane to the Green at Wick.

5 From the edge of the Green, bear left along a narrow lane. In a few yards, at a footpath sign, turn right through a broad gate. Keep the hedge on your left through fields to emerge at a picnic table and pond. Close by is a junction with a road. Cross it and bear left, following the grass verge for 15yds to a lane on the right.

6 Follow this quiet lane, ignoring a right fork, until you reach another lane at Blackhall Cottage. Bear left for 100yds to a junction.

7 Turn right and head downhill along a wooded lane until you meet the River Alun. At a left bend, where the river flows very close to the lane, turn left uphill on a broad path into the woods. Reach a wall and follow it to a small gate. In a few yards, at a fork, take the right-hand path up Old Castle Down. Below on the right is the wooded Cwm Alun. Further on, the path runs alongside a wall to its highest point. Here, beneath you, is the village of St Bride's Major and the headland at Dunraven with the Bristol Channel beyond.

8 Take the path downhill to a track and you soon reach a cattle grid at a lane. Turn right and in a few yards bear left along Pen y Lan Road. At its end, turn left past the Old Vicarage and Pitcott Pool to the start.

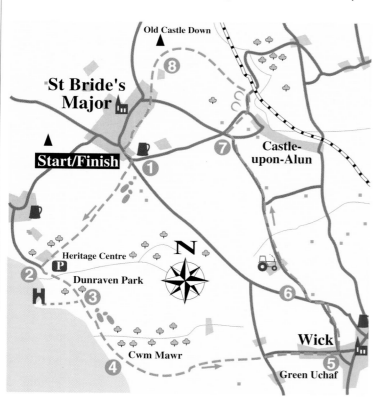

ALONG THE WAY

The precipitous cliffs along the Glamorgan Heritage Coast consist of layers of limestone and shale. At low tide spectacular wave-cut platforms are exposed on the beach.
According to local legend, the Celtic chief Caractacus lived at the promontory fort on Dunraven. Dunraven Castle, a castellated mansion, was knocked down in 1963. More recently, the parkland was opened to the public. Look out for the Blue Lady – a ghost in a blue dress – as you explore Dunraven.

These low, rocky platforms, revealed at low tide, can be seen from point 2

FACT FILE

Distance 8½ miles
Time 3½–4 hours
Map OS Landranger 170
Start Farmer's Arms, St Bride's Major, grid ref 896744
Parking On-street parking in St Bride's Major; car park at Dunraven Bay
Terrain Field, cliff and woodland paths. Quiet lanes
Nearest town Bridgend
Refreshments Farmer's Arms, St Bride's Major; Lamb and Flag Inn, Wick (5 minutes off-route)
Public transport Buses from Bridgend–Llantwit Major stop at the Farmer's Arms
Stiles About twenty, mostly easy
Suitable for Older children, dogs on leads. Take care on cliffs

IRELAND

A Poet's Tower

If you ever have a few hours to spare in Dublin, head for Howth and enjoy a classic coastal cliff walk.

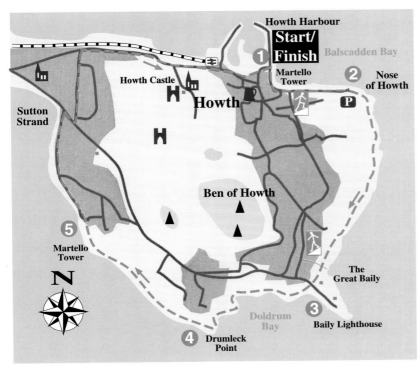

1 Follow the Harbour Road to East Pier, then turn right to walk up Balscadden Road. The road overlooks Balscadden Bay and a Martello tower stands in a good vantage point above the harbour. Follow the road onwards and look out for Balscadden House, where the poet W. B. Yeats lived from 1880 to 1883. 'I have spread my dreams under your feet,' he wrote. 'Tread softly because you tread on my dreams.'

2 Follow the road to its end, where there is a parking space and a few buildings. A well-trodden path leads past some bollards then climbs gently as it turns around the Nose of Howth, with steep and rugged slopes both above and below. When you have rounded the point, you will be able to enjoy views to the Wicklow Mountains. The path descends gradually towards the Baily Lighthouse, at the end of a rocky point. Don't be tempted to take any paths leading inland. Cross over the lighthouse access road and another path leads between bushes to continue; the bushes are garden escapes, adding an exotic flavour to the walk.

3 At one point there is an open view around Doldrum Bay, with the Baily Lighthouse to the left and a white cottage perched on a cliff to the right. The path runs behind the cottage to reach a junction with another path. Turn right and follow this path, but avoid paths leading through gates to right and left. Turn left at another junction of paths and continue to walk gradually downhill. More open slopes are crossed beyond the hedging.

4 After you have rounded Drumleck Point, you will gain views of Dublin Bay. There are short flights of steps and the path runs alongside a stout wall. Later, it crosses a steep and rocky slope, look ahead to spot its course. You will need to keep children and dogs under close control and perhaps use your hands on occasions. An easier path runs to a Martello Tower.

5 Beyond the tower, a clear track leads to a road. Turn left to follow Strand Road, which joins Carrickbrack Road, where a right turn is made. Later, turn left along the road called Offington Park. This leads on to the busy Howth Road, where you turn right to reach the village and harbour where your walk started.

Along the Way

Howth Head dominates Dublin Bay and naturally draws the eye. It is connected to the mainland by a narrow strip of land, and Dublin city has spread across it to make a suburb out of Howth village. The harbour is the starting point for a coastal walk encircling the rugged peninsula with steep cliffs, rocky coves, a lighthouse, Martello towers, birds and exotic plants to be seen en route.

Fact File

Distance 8 miles
Time 4 hours
Maps OSI Discovery 50
Start/parking Howth Harbour, grid ref 288393
Terrain Mostly good cliff paths, but rocky in places
Nearest Town Dublin
Refreshments Around Howth Harbour
Public Transport Frequent Dublin Bus and DART rail services
Stiles None
Suitable for Children and dogs on leads

St Assicus' League

'Six hundred yards in air aloft, six hundred in the deep' is how the
Ballyshanny Poet described Slieve League's cliffs.

1 If you can see the cliffs, you can see which way
to walk from Bunglass. A path follows a fence
from the car park, then continues up over rough
and rocky ground to reach a summit called
Scregeighter. Here you follow a cliff top path
roughly northwards; stay clear of the edge as you
cross the next rise, as the cliffs of the Eagle's Nest
actually overhang at the top.

2 The path descends across a gap and crosses a
hump. Climb steeply uphill for a while, crossing or
passing another hump on the crest. The rocky
ridge of Keeringear has in recent years attracted
the name 'One Man's Pass', though this is really a
feature found later in the walk. The ridge
steepens, and you need to look at your options.

3 In wet weather or strong winds, the safe option
is to omit the ridge, and use a rocky path on the
landward side to by pass any difficulty. You then
take a path uphill which leads on to Slieve
League's summit plateau. In clear dry weather you
should be able to scramble up the rocky ridge if you have a good head for heights.

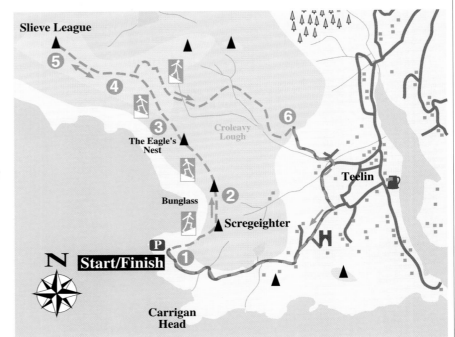

4 The broad, stony plateau is not the true summit of Slieve League, you need to be further north-west. The two broad
summits of the mountain are connected by a ridge which is the original 'One Man's Pass'. There are no difficulties along this
ridge, which is a crest bearing a good path. A rocky climb at the end leads on to the summit, where you head for a large cairn
at 1,972ft. The views can be remarkably extensive, stretching far beyond Co Donegal.

5 Retrace your steps for a while to continue the walk, heading for Slieve League's lower summit. As you follow the path over
the lower summit, keep to the left and walk north-east down a stony slope to all the ruins associated with St Assicus, who spent
seven years on top of Slieve League. Follow the clear pilgrim path downhill, steeply at first, then at a gentler gradient. You will
later reach a small waterfall, and pass Croleavy Lough before reaching a car park.

6 Follow a narrow road down from the car park to reach a junction with another road at a small bridge. Turn right and follow
a narrow road with a central strip of grass, running uphill before dropping to another road. Turn right to follow the road
which you drove along to reach Bunglass. This road twists and turns around Carrigan Head, passing Lough O'Muilligan
before ending back at Bunglass.

Fact File

Distance 9 miles
Time 5 hours
Maps OSI Discovery 10
Start/parking Bunglass, grid ref 558757
Terrain Rugged paths, tracks and roads
Nearest town Carrick
Refreshments Teelin
Public Transport None
Stiles None
Suitable for Hardy hillwalkers

Along the Way

You need to be a determined driver and walker to enjoy Slieve
League. First you must drive along narrow, twisting roads to
reach a car park on a cliff at Bunglass, near Carrick in Co
Donegal, where 2,000ft of rugged, broken, rocky slopes plunge
into the Atlantic. They call this place Radharc Mor – the Big
View – though sometimes it is completely shrouded in mist.

Slieve League seen from Bunglass, the start of the walk

COAST LINE

Belfast Lough features a continuous coastal path between Holywood and Bangor, with views across to the Belfast Hills.

1 Leave the Maypole in the centre of Holywood and walk down Shore Road. Cross the busy dual carriageway, go under the railway, then turn right along the promenade. Pause to identify the Belfast Hills across Belfast Lough, then follow the path onwards.

2 You pass a small pier at Cultra Avenue, then Seafront Road continues along the shore as a gravel track. Rising inland is the Ulster Folk and Transport Museum in the grounds of Cultra Manor. The coast path follows the top of a wall for a short way, then passes Glen Road. A path beside garden walls leads to the next shore road.

3 The path continues alongside a fence bounding a golf course, then runs round a low, rocky wooded point. The path becomes grassy as it continues alongside a wall. There are areas of shingle and rock before the path passes close to a school and rises through an area of scrub. Keep left at a fork in the path, passing a sewage works.

4 The path runs through an arch, then a flight of steps leads up a wooded cliff, before another flight leads back down to the shore. A gravel path by a rocky shore runs into Crawfordsburn Country Park. This is one of the busiest countryside sites in Northern Ireland. You pass a boathouse as you walk around a small bay, and blue waymark arrows on posts indicate the coastal path through the country park.

5 Follow the path through a turnstile and continue along a low cliff on the wooded Grey Point. A sign indicates a diversion to Grey Point Fort, dating from 1904. The path continues around Grey Point and runs through a wood before reaching a road through Helen's Bay. The promenade path around Helen's Bay is a popular walk.

6 A broad track runs over a low, wooded point to continue through Crawfordsburn Country Park. If you have more time to spare, head inland to the Visitor Centre, which has a restaurant on site. After crossing a footbridge, the coast path goes round a rocky, wooded point to continue across a sandy beach.

7 After turning round the next wooded point, the path is concrete for a while, then is tarmac around Swineley Point. Beyond Smelt Mill Bay, the path passes Brompton Road and runs below a tower. After turning around a low cliff, you reach Bangor. The harbour area features plenty of amenities and a marina. Head inland to Castle Green, where buses and trains run back to Holywood.

ALONG THE WAY

Look out for the enormous maypole in the centre of Holywood. There has been one on this site since at least the early 18th century. The Ulster Folk and Transport Museum is well worth a visit but perhaps on a different day to your walk as there's so much to see. Crawfordsburn Country Park is one of the busiest countryside centres in Northern Ireland with plenty of fascinating background material to the area.

FACT FILE

Distance 10 miles
Time 5 hours
Map OSNI Discoverer 15
Start Holywood, grid ref 398793
Parking Holywood, Helen's Bay, Crawfordsburn and Bangor
Terrain Simple coastal walking on firm paths and minor roads
Nearest towns Holywood and Bangor
Refreshments Pubs and cafés in Holywood and Bangor. Restaurant in Crawfordsburn Country Park Visitor Centre. Coaching inn in Crawfordsburn village
Public Transport Ulsterbus and Northern Ireland Railways
Stiles None
Suitable for Children, dogs on leads

SOUTH EAST

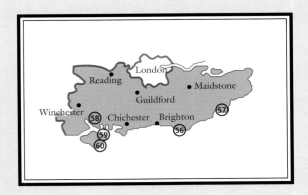

HEAD FOR HEIGHTS

Your reward on this challenging walk along the sea cliffs of Sussex is the sight of some of the most dramatic landscape in the south.

1 Take the gravel track (which runs behind the lavatories). Go through a wooden gate and within a few yards turn left and soon join a wide grassy path which leads mercilessly over three of the challenging Seven Sisters tackled on this walk. Be alert for a memorial known as the Sarsen Stone situated at the rise of the third sister.

2 From the stone, go downhill and at the bottom leave the coastal path and turn right along the gap. There is no marker post for this path which is initially hard to define, but it soon identifies itself as a bridleway and becomes a wide grassy track. Ignore a stile on the left and maintain direction. The grass gives way to gravel as you enter the cluster of houses that make up Crowlink.

3 With Crowlink House on your left go right uphill, heading for a stile. Maintain direction over the springy downland turf to go through a wooden gate. Now head downhill between two clumps of trees to reach a double stone stile. Take the left option to cross a field and then follow a steep path downhill. Go right through a gate to enter the village of East Dean.

4 Turn left to walk through the village and join the main road. Go right and then take the path on your right opposite the garage. This will soon bring you to the village green and the Tiger Inn. Continue ahead by the green and then turn left along a road signed to Birling Gap. The Church of St Simon and St Jude is on the left and well worth a short visit. At the T junction turn right along the road, which is quite busy but has a more than adequate grassy verge. Cross the road opposite the Seven Sisters Sheep Centre and walk up the drive to Birling Manor. Don't enter the house grounds but go left through a gate. At a second gate where the path forks keep ahead with a small spinney on your right. Go through another gate and turn right.

5 As you approach Cornish Farm join a concrete drive which passes to the north of the farm buildings. Ignore a waymarked path on the left and immediately after going through a metal gate climb diagonally right up the hillside. As the ascent levels out, continue ahead aiming for a gate in the hedge. Don't go through the gate but turn left to enjoy a beautiful stretch of downland before reaching a road.

6 Walk to the right as far as the wall perimeter then cross the road and continue ahead over the grassy downland. The descent is at first gentle but becomes quite steep as you join the South Downs Way to its starting point on the outskirts of Eastbourne.

7 At the road, take the gravel path by the side of the small café. As the gravel peters out, bear left and follow the path that skirts the edge of the cliffs. At the bottom of a flight of steps where the path forks, take the lower route. There is a pleasant detour which leads down to the beach through Cow Gap with an informative notice board explaining the unique geology of the area. The main path soon widens and the impressive outline of Beachy Head dominates the skyline. The ascent is demanding but soon achieved and once at the top you rejoin the South Downs Way.

8 As you continue following the cliff top path the Belle Tout Lighthouse provides a focal point. The path swings around the perimeter of the lighthouse before regaining the cliff edge. Birling Gap and the Seven Sisters are now visible in the distance – a satisfying reminder of what has been achieved.

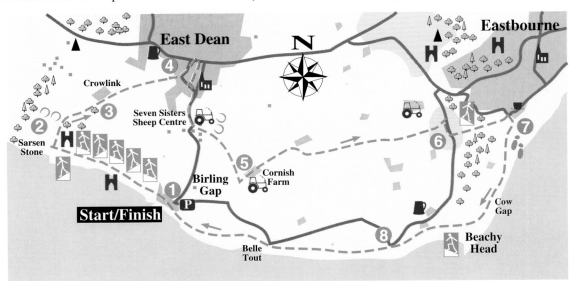

FACT FILE

Distance 11 miles
Time 5 hours
Map OS Landranger 199, OS Pathfinder 1
Start/parking Birling Gap car park, grid ref 554960
Terrain Good underfoot but with some very steep sections
Nearest town Eastbourne

Refreshments Birling Gap Hotel, the Tiger Inn at East Dean, café at the start of South Downs Way and Beachy Head Hotel. Excellent picnic spots en route
Public transport BR at Eastbourne. 711/712 Coastline Bus between Brighton and Eastbourne stops at East Dean from where you could start the walk. Telephone 01323 727354

Stiles Three
Suitable for Older children, dogs on leads

ALONG THE WAY

This treacherous coastline has been responsible for the wreck of many vessels and in the early 18th century a local parson is said to have hollowed out a cave in the cliff face, where on stormy nights he would light a lantern to guide stricken sailors to safety. The Belle Tout lighthouse was erected in 1834 but soon proved to be impractical, being shrouded in mist for much of the year. The present red and white lighthouse was built below Beachy Head in 1902 and its light can be seen for up to 16 miles.

The Seven Sisters viewed from Birling Gap

POWER AND GLORY

Experience the splendid isolation of Britain's longest shingle beach.

1 Before setting off take a few minutes to read the information boards explaining the history and natural history of the area. You can choose whether to walk along the waterline, the shingle beach or even the road. Whichever route you choose head in a southerly direction and if necessary rejoin the road by the Pilot Inn.

2 The footpath leads through the car park and across the shingle before joining a narrow lane. Walk left, passing the lifeboat station and eventually the new lighthouse. Follow the lane around to the right to approach the old lighthouse and the perimeter of the power station. Follow the path alongside the power station wall towards the shoreline.

3 The mean high water line indicates the course of the path across the ever-changing shingle and provides a stimulating walk with views out over the channel to the left and Denge Marsh on your right. When you reach a coastguard lookout leave the shingle to join a rough track on the right.

4 As you walk along this track you may be lucky enough to see a hen-harrier on its low-level hunting flight. There is the boundary of a military firing range on your left, but this doesn't detract from the tranquillity of your surroundings. The rough track soon gives way to concrete and as you reach

the limit of the military fencing look for a metal gate on your right. Go through the gate and follow the path over a small bridge and then through a wooden gate. Turn right and follow the bank of Dengemarsh Sewer to approach a fence over a ditch. Turn left and follow the ditch which forms the perimeter of pasture land. At the top of the field go left, still following the boundary, until you reach a lagoon. Go right to join a wide gravel track which leads past an entrance to the RSPB reserve.

5 When you reach a metal gate go left, following a newly-signed footpath to Lydd. You can see All Saints Church at Lydd, with its 130ft tower clearly visible over the marshes. Ignore a path joining from the right and keep ahead to follow the edge of a dyke. Bear left over a bridge into a field. Cross the field, aiming for a metal bridge leading over a ditch. Once over this bridge keep ahead to join a lane.

6 Turn right to walk into Lydd. Keep ahead at a fork and again at a junction. To explore Lydd turn left at the roundabout. Otherwise continue along the road and take the path on the right opposite the cemetery. Bear diagonally left at the double electricity poles; cross a footbridge and continue ahead, aiming for a distinctive yellow marker post in the hedge opposite. Turn right along the perimeter of the field before crossing a bridge on your left. Follow the path towards a railway crossing. Don't cross the line here but walk to the right to cross it using two high ladder stiles. Maintain your direction over a wide wooden bridge and skirt the edge of the runway at Lydd Airport. Climb a stile on the left and, leaving the railway line, cross a footbridge to join a wide, fenced path through the shingle.

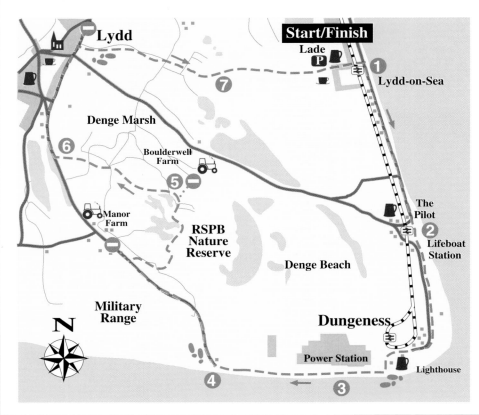

7 Be alert for two low, concrete footpath signs on either side of the path and go right through the fence. There is no obvious path over the shingle and this could be a good time to practise your navigational skills – why not take a bearing before setting out? There is another small concrete marker part-way across this mile of open shingle and as an additional aid you should be aiming in the direction of a small yellow hut just visible in the distance. You should reach a disused railway line opposite two stiles. Cross the line and walk towards the last bungalow on your left. Join a road and keep ahead to arrive back at the car park.

FACT FILE

Distance 11½ miles
Time 5 hours
Maps OS Landranger 189, OS Pathfinder 1272
Start/parking Lade car park, grid ref 085212
Terrain Field paths and some minor roads but with long stretches over shingle. Although flat, this is a demanding walk
Nearest town Lydd
Refreshments Pub at start/finish. Further options at Dungeness and in Lydd
Public transport The Romney Hythe and Dymchurch Railway runs a regular service to Dungeness on weekends in March and October and daily in summer. Tel 01797 362353. Lydd and Dungeness are served by Stagecoach East Kent. Tel 01303 253118
Stiles Eight
Suitable for Older children and dogs

ALONG THE WAY

Although the power station sited on the tip of Denge Marsh is never far away, this isolated shingle promontory supports a wide range of plant life, including many rare species. The gravel pits are a haven for migratory and breeding colonies of birds with the RSPB sanctuary at Boulderswell providing 12,000 acres of protected habitat. There has been a lighthouse on the promontory since the 17th century but the ever-shifting shingle quickly made these early structures obsolete. The modern lighthouse was built in 1961 because the existing one was overshadowed by the new power station.

The shingle beach explored on this walk is an ideal place to get away from it all

GATEWAY TO THE WORLD

Enjoy glimpses of the Hamble river before you join the Solent Way on the shores of bustling Southampton Water.

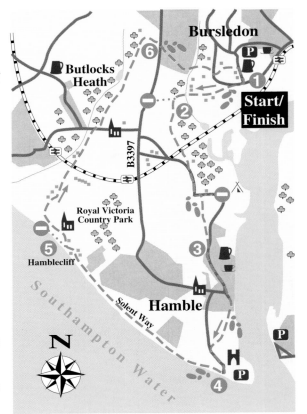

1 From the station car park head up the slope (signposted Jolly Sailor). Veer left at the top for the inn or right into Bursledon High Street for the main circuit. Bear half-left at the telephone box, pass the Vine and Salterns Lane and continue into Kew Lane. Go straight on as the lane bends right and follow a path to a section of driveway. Join a path running to the left of a white house, descend to a stream and follow the path through woodland (Mallards Moor). Soon the path curves left to a concrete drive.

2 Turn right for several yards, then swing half-left and follow a path beside a high wire fence. Bear sharp left at the fence corner, avoid a right turning, cross the railway and continue to the road by the entrance to Wessex Manor. Follow the road ahead, bend sharp left, then turn right to follow a path across the fields. Pass gardens and houses, climb a slope and turn left by some silver birch trees. Follow the path down to the road and turn right.

3 Pass the entrance to Hamble Marina. When the road bends sharp right, in the centre of Hamble, take the road on the left down between the Georgian cottages and pubs to the public 'hard' (quay) and foreshore. Continue along the road beside the Bugle Inn and bear right, up the hill, by Sydney Cottages. Turn left at a pretty green and follow the path over a footbridge into the woodland. Emerge from the trees and look for a kissing gate ahead. Cross the field, with a fence on your left, to the next gate and continue for a few yards to a junction. Turn right and follow the path across Hamble Common to a parking area. Bear left immediately before the road and follow a path parallel to the road.

4 At the entrance to Hamble Point Marina cross to the car park on the edge of Southampton Water. Turn right on to the Solent Way. Pass the anti-aircraft gun emplacement and follow the path beside the water. Further on, join the sea wall and follow it alongside the BP oil terminal. Continue on a stretch of beach, veering right at a concrete fortification, through some trees to the road. Turn left, passing a sign for Westfield Common. At the next junction, keep to the right of Hamblecliff House and then to the left of Hamblecliff Stables. Follow the path beside Netley Sailing Club, swing right and head through the trees to the Royal Victoria Country Park.

5 From the entrance to the old chapel turn right, then right at the next junction. Take the path to the left of the Empire Room and keep the car park on the left. Join the main drive and follow it down to Hound Road. Keep going to the next main junction. Turn right, then look for a footpath sign. Head for a stile and cross the field with woodland on the left. Continue across the fields, crossing four stiles. Bear right at a fence corner. Cross open ground to some traffic lights and go straight over.

6 Take the first right turn and pass St Paul's church on the left. Follow the road round to the left and into Foundry Crescent. Veer right and right again by the adventure playground. Follow the path alongside a stream and bear left at the next junction of paths. Cross a footbridge and a road and continue as the path climbs to the next road. Keep going for a few yards, turn left through a gate and follow a path between paddocks. Turn right at the next road and bear left into Bursledon High Street. Go left again into Station Hill and retrace your steps to the car park.

Visit the pretty village of Hamble at point 3 of this walk

FACT FILE

Distance 9 miles
Time 4 hours
Map OS Landranger 196, OS Outdoor Leisure 22
Start/parking Public car park at Bursledon railway station, grid ref 488095
Terrain Some roads, field and woodland paths, stretches of sea wall and beach. Muddy in some places
Nearest town Southampton
Refreshments The Jolly Sailor and The Vine at Bursledon. Several pubs in Hamble and refreshments at the Royal Victoria Country Park
Public transport Train services between Bournemouth, Southampton, Fareham and Portsmouth, stopping at Bursledon. Various bus operators run local services and Hampshire County Council in Winchester publishes a public transport map
Stiles Five
Suitable for Children and dogs

ALONG THE WAY

This area has several claims to fame. The Hamble River, together with Bursledon's Jolly Sailor and the neighbouring Elephant Boatyard, regularly appeared in the television sailing soap *Howard's Way*. It was from Hamble Common that Henry VIII watched in horror as his famous flagship, the 91-gun Mary Rose, sank with the loss of 700 men just off the nearby coast in 1545. The Royal Victoria Country Park was once home to Britain's largest military hospital. Opened in 1863, this huge building was over 400yds long and included 1,000 beds. The sick, dying and injured were brought here from the war-torn corners of the British Empire. The hospital was demolished in 1966 but the chapel, with its distinctive dome, remains and includes a fascinating heritage centre.

POWER OF THE WIND

Follow the coastline to Culver Cliff, where there are stunning views across to Spithead, and then head across open countryside to visit the Isle of Wight's only surviving windmill.

1 Make for the seaward end of Bembridge Harbour, leave the B3395 road and take the Coastal Path (signposted Foreland). Follow the path between trees and hedgerows and you soon reach a junction with a wide drive. Turn left and then right. To avoid the beach, follow the drives or pathways running parallel to the shore, then rejoin the main path at the lifeboat station. Follow the woodland path to reach the edge of the beach. Head along the shoreline towards the lifeboat station and look for a flight of steps on the right, running up to a footpath sign. Bear left and follow the path. Draw level with the lifeboat station and continue beside some seats.

2 Beyond a road and drive, follow the path between fences and hedges. Eventually you come to a drive opposite a bungalow, Green End. Turn left here and curve right at the Foreland Farm Lane sign. Bear left at the next Coastal Path sign and swing right at the end of the road, by the coastguard station. Pass to the left of the Crab and Lobster Inn and look for the path running along the grassy headland. Pass a parking area and paddock and keep on the path. Turn left at a junction of paths, then bear right and walk through some woodland. Pass a sign for Whitecliff Bay. Further on the walk skirts the playing fields of Bembridge School before descending a flight of steps into more woodland.

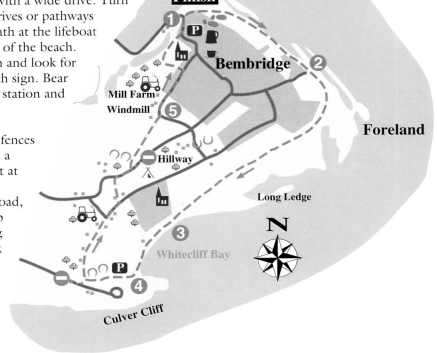

3 Continue along the path, with glimpses of Whitecliff Bay between the trees – close by is a caravan park. Cross a suspension bridge, pass a café and go alongside some wooden chalets on the edge of open fields. Bear left through an opening in the hedgerow, just before several more chalets, and follow the paved path up the slope to a stile. Keep on the path and head for the monument on Culver Down.

4 With your back to the monument and Culver Cliff, walk down the slope between bushes until you come to a clear path. Follow it down to the foot of the hillside and bear right to a stile. Head along the track to the stile in the next boundary, then go straight on along a quiet lane to the next road junction. Turn right and follow the road; turn left into Common Wood Lane and you will see the buildings of Bembridge Airport. Turn right at the next junction, then left after several minutes to join a bridleway, signposted to Bembridge Windmill. Follow the track through woodland, then up a slope to the windmill. When you reach the road at a bend, head towards Bembridge.

5 Follow the road for almost ½ mile, then bear left at a footpath sign for the Point. Descend the slope and at the bottom turn right. Follow the path through woodland and join a track running between houses and apartments. Pass the Row Barge inn. Beyond it you are back on the edge of Bembridge Harbour.

A tranquil waterside scene on this Isle of Wight walk

FACT FILE

Distance 6 miles
Time 2½ hours
Maps OS Landranger 196, OS Outdoor Leisure 29
Start/parking Bembridge Harbour, grid ref 642886
Terrain Coastal and field paths, tracks and some stretches of road
Nearest town Sandown
Refreshments The Row Barge, Bembridge Harbour, the Crab and Lobster, Foreland
Public transport Southern Vectis run buses to and from Bembridge Harbour, tel 01983 522456
Stiles Three
Suitable for Children and dogs. To walk along the beach at Bembridge, it is advisable to obtain a copy of the tide table from local newsagents or telephone the Harbour Master on 01983 872828

ALONG THE WAY

Bembridge Harbour is a busy, colourful place and very much a centre for sailing. On its northern side is St Helen's Duver, a peaceful haven of grassland, sand dunes and rare flowers. On top of Culver Down, 343ft above the sea, is a monument dedicated to Charles Anderson Pelham, Earl of Yarborough and First Commodore of the Royal Yacht Squadron. From the obelisk there are magnificent views over the south-east corner of the island towards Spithead. Bembridge Windmill, which dates back to 1700, is in the care of the National Trust and contains much of its original wooden machinery. It is open to visitors between April and October – tel 01983 873945.

A Medieval Pepper Pot

Much of the Isle of Wight can be seen on this superb walk which follows part of the island's popular coastal path.

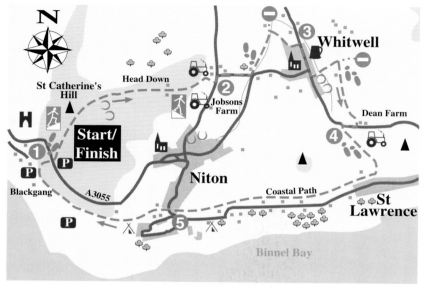

1 Cross the A3055 to a stile and go up the steep slope towards St Catherine's Oratory. Further up, look for a line of pylons and a stile in the fence. Cross over, then veer slightly right to another stile. With the tower on your left go to the next stile and, a few yards further on, cross the next stile by an old white trig point. Turn left and follow the field edge. Make for a stile in the field corner and bear right. Head for a gate on the far side of the field and join a path running between fences and hedgerows. Pass several path junctions and join a track through a tunnel of trees. Pass Hillside Farm and follow the track (Crocker Lane) to the road.

2 Turn left, take the first right turning (Kingates Lane) and follow it between trees and hedgerows. Take the path on the left immediately beyond the entrance to a house called Copperfields. Pass over a junction of routes, cross a stile and footbridge into a field and continue ahead. Pass a solitary footpath sign, cross a stile in the field corner and keep going for about 50yds. Bear right over a stile and footbridge, turn left and cross several more stiles and footbridges. Keep alongside the stream and at one point cross a track. Follow the path to a drive and turn right. Bear left at the next junction, opposite some bungalows, and walk down to the next junction.

3 Turn right and walk through Whitwell. Pass the White Horse Inn, Kemming Road and the church and continue, following the main street towards St Lawrence until you reach a bridleroad signposted to Wroxall. Go through a gate and keep a fence on the left. Cross a field boundary and continue beside the fence to the next gate. Bear right and follow the path through the trees and across a disused railway line. Pass through another gate and head across the grassy slopes to a footpath sign. Turn right (signposted Dean Farm) and pass between stone cottages. Go through a gate, over a stile and across a rectangular field. Aim for the gate in the far boundary and follow a track curving left. Approach the buildings of Dean Farm, go through a gate, turn right and walk down to the road.

4 Turn right and just before the bend bear left at the sign for Niton Radio Maritime Services. Follow the tarmac lane to the point where it bends sharp right. Go straight ahead over a stile and walk down to the route of the Coastal Path. Turn right and follow the cliff top path to Niton. Eventually you reach a wall; drop down a slope to merge with a drive. Turn left for Blackgang and Westcliff and head for the road at Niton.

5 Turn right for several steps, then bear sharp left to rejoin the Coastal Path. Follow a drive, swinging right at the entrance to some properties. Head up through a tunnel of trees to a field. Continue along the Coastal Path and soon the distinctive outline of St Catherine's Lighthouse looms into view. Follow the path as it climbs high over the downs. Further on, the path descends towards the amusement park at Blackgang Chine. Bear sharp right and follow it away from the sea, returning to the car park.

Fact File

Distance 7½ miles
Time 3 hours
Maps OS Landranger 196, OS Outdoor Leisure 29
Start/parking Public car park at Blackgang, grid ref 491767

Terrain Field paths and tracks, some stretches of road, cliff top path
Nearest town Ventnor
Refreshments The White Horse Inn, Whitwell; the Buddle Inn and White Lion, Niton
Public transport Southern Vectis

operates several services in the area. Tel 01983 522456
Stiles Seventeen
Suitable for Children and dogs

The lighthouse at St Catherine's Point – the southernmost tip of the Isle of Wight

ALONG THE WAY

The Pepper Pot, an unusual octagonal tower which comes into view at different stages of this walk, is all that remains of a medieval lighthouse or beacon. It was built by Walter de Godeton as an act of penance for receiving casks of wine smuggled ashore from a wrecked ship on the nearby coast in 1314. Attached to the lighthouse was a chapel or oratory where a priest would tend the light and pray for the souls of those lost at sea. Much of the Isle of Wight is visible from here, 780ft above the sea. The lighthouse at St Catherine's Point was built in 1838 following the wrecking of the 345-ton *Clarendon*, which was driven ashore here during a violent storm. The lighthouse represents the southernmost point of the Isle of Wight.

SOUTH WEST

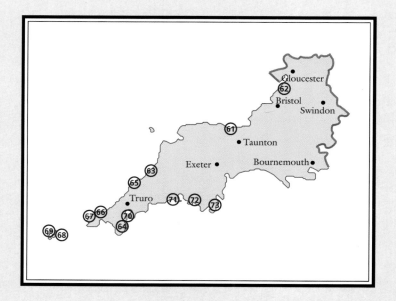

A LOST DALLAS

Explore the quiet Somerset coastline east of Watchet, an intriguing landscape with cliff top paths, crumbling rock faces, pebbly beaches and a real sense of history.

1 Follow Sea Lane back towards the A39 for ½ mile to Meadow House Hotel, passing the ruins of Kilve Chantry and St Mary's Church. Follow the lane on the left opposite the hotel for 200yds, then bear left on to a gravelled track. This track soon enters an open field where almost immediately you cross a stile on the right.

2 Follow a field path across four fields to reach Lower Hill Farm. In the first three fields, the path borders woodland, then crosses a paddock to reach a crosstrack by the house. Turn left and pass in front of Lower Hill Farm, before taking a signposted path into arable fields. Follow the right-hand hedgerow across the first two fields, enjoying the views of the Bristol Channel. Cross a third field to reach the lane in Kilton.

3 Turn left and follow the lane through Kilton to St Nicholas Church (the detour is obligatory). Continue north along this quiet lane to Lilstock, where you pass the redundant St Andrew's Church on the right as you enter the village. Continue through Lilstock to Lilstock Farm.

4 Just beyond the farm, turn left and follow the track northwards to the beach parking area. On reaching the coast, turn left and follow the coast path for 2½ miles back to Kilve beach. Here a left turn takes you back to the car park. The coast path above the cliffs is unfenced, so take care.

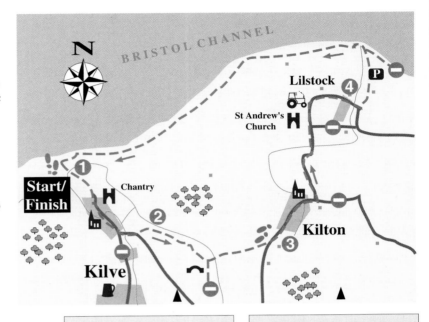

The final stretch of the walk takes you along the cliff tops to Kilve beach

ALONG THE WAY

The underlying shale in this corner of Somerset holds more than five million gallons of oil, and the 1920s Kilve had aspirations of becoming a booming oil town. An oil retort house is all that remains of this episode in the village's history. In earlier times there was a chantry in Kilve, the ivy-clad ruins of which can still be seen by the road below the church. It was destroyed by fire in 1850, and the blue coloration of the flames confirmed local suspicions that it was a hotbed of liquor smuggling. The oil magnates and the smugglers have long since gone, leaving a peaceful corner of Somerset for today's walker to enjoy.

FACT FILE

Distance 5 miles
Time 2–3 hours
Maps OS Landranger 181, OS Pathfinder ST 04/14
Start/parking Turn off the A39 Bridgwater to Minehead road by the Hood Arms in Kilve into Sea Lane. The beach car park lies at the end of this cul-de-sac, grid ref 145443
Terrain Undulating countryside and coastline
Nearest town Watchet
Refreshments The Hood Arms in Kilve
Public transport Southern National Buses running between Bridgwater and Minehead pass through Kilve
Stiles Five easy wooden stiles
Suitable for Active adults and children and well-controlled dogs

BESIDE THE SEVERN SEA

The attractive village of Berkeley is the starting point for a walk which includes an imposing castle and a deer park – but the Severn is the dominant theme and whether you're interested in birds or boats, you'll need your binoculars.

1 Walk east along the main street (Salter St/Canonbury St) then turn left on a footpath to Halmore. Keep straight on, soon crossing the B4066. When you reach a railway (freight only) turn left as far as a house, then cross the line and continue across fields. Aim at first for the far corner of a wood, then go diagonally right to pass to the right of Wanswell Court Farm. There are two lines of pylons to your right – go through a gate about 100yds before the pylons, then continue by the hedge, with the farm a field's width to your left.

2 Go through a gate in the corner of the field and keep straight on to Halmore Lane. The path continues opposite, along the right-hand field-edge for 50yds. Climb a stile, go through an iron gate and then straight on over a field, with a hedge on your left.

3 Cross a ditch, stile and barbed-wire fence, then go diagonally across a field. Follow the hedge past Acton Hall Farm before climbing a stile and going diagonally left to the far corner of another field. Turn left along a green lane to reach a metalled lane at Brookend. Turn right, then left at a junction.

4 When you reach the main road at Sharpness you join the Severn Way. Our onward route is to the left, but a detour to the right will enable you to see more of the docks and visit the point where the Gloucester and Sharpness Ship Canal joins the river. The canal was opened in 1827 to allow ships to bypass the treacherous Severn. Resuming the walk, head south on the Severn Way. Soon after you pass the Pier View Hotel a right turn takes you across the freight line to the B4066. Turn right and then shortly afterwards left to the docks and the river. Walk south along the floodbank.

5 After a mile you come to a creek, Berkeley Pill. Follow it to the road near Berkeley, then turn right towards the power station (now being decommissioned). The footpath skirts the Nuclear Electric site and returns to the Severn. Walk south, first along the floodbank, then on a concrete breakwater.

6 About 1½ miles after passing a small wood, turn left by a creek. Leave the Severn Way and join a bridleway which runs alongside the creek. After a further ½ mile you reach a junction. Turn left initially, then fork right, joining a thickly hedged track.

7 Turn left along a lane. After ½ mile turn right on a bridleway which skirts Bevington Hill. Turn right on another lane, then go straight on through Bevington Farm. Pass through the far left of four gates, following a

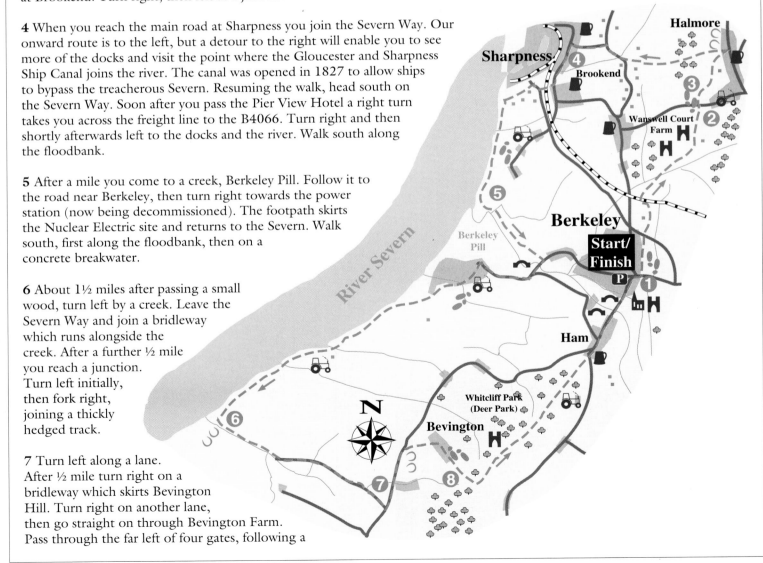

clear track which runs close to the wall of Whitcliff Park for a while, before it veers away to climb gently to the top of a long, low ridge.

8 After going through a gate fork left, and before long you pass a house. Look for a stile which takes you over the wall into Whitcliff Park, first enclosed as a deer park in the 13th century. A permissive path has recently been created, and is shown on a map by the wall. You can either follow this or the existing right of way, which goes along the top of the ridge, eventually joining an avenue of trees before it descends to a field. Go straight on, through Ham, to reach Berkeley. As you enter the village a footpath allows a good view of the castle (open to the public in summer). Not far away, by the churchyard, you can see the home of Edward Jenner, who discovered the smallpox vaccine. The house is now a museum, also open only in summer.

From Whitcliff Park you can see across the Severn Vale to the Cotswolds

ALONG THE WAY

This is a walk of some contrasts, and one surprise – who would expect to find big ships and busy docks in rural Gloucestershire? Yet that is exactly what you will see at Sharpness, where the Gloucester and Sharpness Ship Canal joins the Severn. Elsewhere the peace of the Vale remains undisturbed, whether you're walking beside the river or along one of the lovely green lanes which are a feature of Severnside. Towards the end of the walk there are good views of Berkeley Castle, the home of the Berkeley family for over 800 years. The castle has witnessed many notable events, but the one which most grips the imagination of visitors is the brutal murder of Edward II in 1327.

Look out for herons while walking in the Severn Vale

FACT FILE

Distance 15 miles
Time 6½ hours
Maps OS Landranger 162, OS Outdoor Leisure 14
Start Salter Street, Berkeley, grid ref 684993
Parking In Berkeley – follow signs from Salter Street
Terrain Flat, pastoral landscape subject to flooding and always muddy in places

Nearest town Dursley
Refreshments Fair choice in Berkeley; pubs at Sharpness and Ham
Public transport Badgerline bus 308 Bristol–Gloucester stops on Salter Street, Monday–Saturday only (for enquiries call 0117 553231); nearest rail station is Cam and Dursley (5 miles)
Stiles A few, also an electric fence and a couple of locked gates
Suitable for Older children and fit dogs

POET'S PARADISE

Sample the rugged and remote beauty of the North Cornwall coast that provided inspiration for Thomas Hardy.

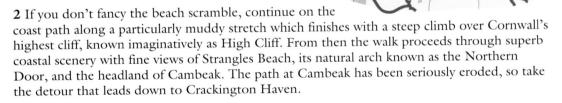

1 Park at Boscastle and walk down towards the harbour. Pick up the coast path by the Witchcraft Museum and follow it out on to the headland and then along the coast, passing the fine coastal waterfall at Pentargon Cove. The path ahead is quite exposed and if you have children with you, you will need to take extra care here. At Fire Beacon Point the path heads briefly inland before climbing steeply to Rusey Cliff.

2a For the adventurous, a beach scramble from Rusey Cliff to Strangles Beach is an exciting alternative to the coast path at low tide. You only occasionally need to use your hands, although the final climb along and down from Voter Run is quite exposed and a short rope could be useful. The coast path drops down steeply from Rusey Cliff. Detour off the path to follow the crumbling ridge down to the sea. Alternatively, a little further on there is a faint path marked out in its lower stages by white rocks. This leads down to the coast by a red life-saving buoy. Pick your way along Rusey Beach to the headland, Voter Run. Scramble out as far as possible along the headland and then back inland along the arete. An exposed crack leads down off the headland. From here head on to Strangles Beach. Take the steep path that leads back to the coast path.

2 If you don't fancy the beach scramble, continue on the coast path along a particularly muddy stretch which finishes with a steep climb over Cornwall's highest cliff, known imaginatively as High Cliff. From then the walk proceeds through superb coastal scenery with fine views of Strangles Beach, its natural arch known as the Northern Door, and the headland of Cambeak. The path at Cambeak has been seriously eroded, so take the detour that leads down to Crackington Haven.

3 Take the road out of Crackington Haven and follow the track signposted to East Wood. Carry on through the gate at Ludon Vean and cross into a wood by way of the bridge. Immediately the path forks. Take the right-hand path, cross another bridge and then turn left. The path follows a delightful stream. Turn right at the crossroads up the muddy track and follow the steep path that leads between gorse bushes to the farmhouse at Trevigue.

4 Return to the coast path and back over High Cliff to Rusey Cliff. Take the path inland and turn right on to the far track. Turn right on to the lane, follow it and then go left to a set of farm buildings. Take the second signposted footpath to Trebyla Farm. Turn right on to the farm track and the path opposite over a series of stiles to Trewannett Farm. Turn right past the Rectory. Follow the track left. At the crossroads take the right-hand path past the cottage. The path finishes at a road. Almost immediately a track forks left. Take this as it returns to a footpath and leads through the Valency Valley back to the beginning of the walk.

FACT FILE

Distance 14 miles
Time 7 hours
Map OS Landranger 190
Start/parking Boscastle, grid ref 101913
Terrain Coast path, woodland, optional beach scramble
Nearest towns Boscastle/ Crackington Haven
Refreshments Variety in Boscastle, café at Crackington Haven, National Trust guest house and coffee shop at Trevigue
Public transport Local buses run to Boscastle and Crackington Haven
Stiles Several
Suitable for Active walkers

ALONG THE WAY

This wild and remote part of Cornwall holds a special attraction for fans of Thomas Hardy – he celebrated this magnificent area in his novel *A Pair of Blue Eyes* and in much of his finest poetry. The walk takes you past the Rectory where he met his first wife, Emma Gifford. The coast is a haven for seals and many breeds of seabird.

COAST AND RIVER

This beautiful walk offers splendid coastal scenery and sheltered wooded valleys beside the river, returning across unspoilt countryside and quiet lanes.

1 With the sea to your left, take the coastal footpath to the right of the car park. Follow the well-defined path. At Rosemullion Head (signed), bear left around the headland.

2 After the headland climb the stile and skirt the grassy field along the cliff top. At the end of the field cross the stream on a wooden bridge, then go over the stile to the next field. Follow the path and continue through Mawnan Glebe Woods, then along the field edge and on to the rocky footpath around Toll Point.

3 Pass through a kissing gate and head downhill to the next kissing gate and across the back of the beach. Continue behind the boathouse, on to the next beach. At the end of the second beach go up the slipway in front of the boathouse and immediately over the stile. When the path forks about 150yds after Bosloe keep left to the next stile, continue up the field and emerge on the road. Turn left and walk down into Durgan.

4 With the Old School House on the left, turn right to pass Post Box Cottage on your left. Walk up the lane for about 50yds, then turn left opposite Chyandour Cottage and rejoin the coastal path. After a short distance climb some wooden steps and continue. Walk behind the next beach with Trebah Gardens on your right and go through the kissing gate. A

short distance up, the coastal footpath on your left (signed) continues to Helford Passage.

5 At the road turn right. Walk to the top of the hill to a T junction. Turn left and continue on the narrow road to the last house, Green Ace, where a public footpath sign points across the field to your left. Head diagonally down the field and just before the bottom corner two posts mark the exit on your left. Turn right on the tarmac lane. At the road turn left then almost immediately right on to the farm lane signposted Lower Penpol.

6 Follow the lane, which is at first straight then bends left and right. Go through a gate, past the last farm building on your left. Continue straight along the edge of the next two fields. At the cottage, turn right down the lane. After about 100yds, opposite the Old Orchard, turn left over the stile. Walk through two more fields then, in the third, skirt the hill to a stone stile on the left. Cross the stile and walk up between fences to a road. Cross the road and go straight ahead to the next road. Turn left to Mawnan Smith square.

7 At the T junction turn right then take the next right into Carlidnack Road. Continue to Carlidnack Lane, where you turn right. When the lane makes a sharp left at a house called Pendine continue straight ahead downhill. At a white gate bear right into the woods. At a signpost for Maenporth turn right over the bridge then over a stile crossing two streams. Turn left out of the woods and go straight ahead – ignore the blue marker signs. At a wooden signpost emerge on a road with the car park ahead.

FACT FILE

Distance 11 miles
Time 5½ hours
Map OS Landranger 204
Start/parking Maenporth beach car park, grid ref 790296
Terrain Mostly well-defined paths, can be muddy in places
Nearest town Falmouth
Refreshments Varied at Mawnan Smith. Ferry Boat Inn at Helford
Public transport None
Stiles Many, stone or wood, easy
Suitable for Older children, dogs on leads

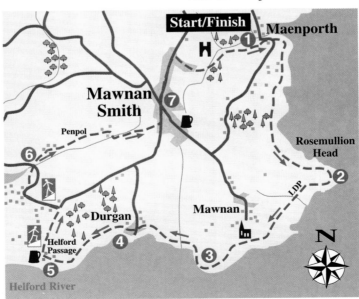

ALONG THE WAY

When you have lingered over the view from Rosemullion Head there is still plenty to discover. The sheltered Helford River provides a safe mooring for a colourful array of boats and you pass two famous gardens, Trebah and Glendurgan.

The fishing hamlet of Durgan has been preserved by the National Trust. Wall plaques identify the former use of the buildings.

Stop at Helford Passage and watch the passenger ferry, in operation since 1801, crossing the river here.

CHURCH AND COAST

Follow part of the North Cornwall coast with an optional visit to a
well-known landmark at Bedruthan Steps.

1 Leave the car park by the gates, turn left and follow the road around. Bear left, keeping Trerair Farm on your right. Ahead of you is the Atlantic Ocean with Trevose Head prominent. After ½ mile turn right (signed Penrose) walk down the steep hill, over the bridge and up the hill to enter the tiny village.

2 Turn left at the T junction in Penrose. At the top of the rise, ignore the footpaths to the right and left and continue on the metalled road down to a wooded valley. Continue uphill and in just over ½ mile turn left at a T junction, signed to Porthcothan.

3 From here the views of the Atlantic coast are superb. In ½ mile turn left at a T junction on to the B3276, signed to Newquay, and walk downhill for about 1 mile to reach the popular bay and sandy beach at Porthcothan.

4 After crossing Porthcothan bridge (beware of traffic) and admiring the Atlantic breakers, you have a choice: either continue uphill along the road to point 5 or take the coast path.

4a To follow the coast path, turn right and walk along the sandy path by the Post Office and Stores; entering the dunes bear left, look for the Acorn sign and walk up the cliffside path.

4b You soon reach the cove at Porth Mear. From here the coast path ascends to overlook High Cove and continues towards Park Head.

4c You may opt to walk around the Head (adding to your mileage and time) or aim directly for Pentire Steps, following the clearly defined steep paths past Diggory's Island and Queen Bess Rock (now alas without her head!) to reach Carnewas Cliff, perhaps better known as Bedruthan Steps. From the car park follow the lane turning right to rejoin the main road at 6.

5 If you are following the B3276 road route, walk up the steep hill out of Porthcothan and in ½ mile turn right at the top, following the sign for Bedruthan and Newquay.

6 Continue along the road with its ever-changing views of coast and countryside to the road to Carnewas Cliff, where a short diversion can be made to view the cliff staircase. Here the road and the optional coast walks meet to continue to the village of Trenance with the Bedruthan Steps Hotel.

7 At the next road junction leave the B3276 and bear left (signed St Eval) to pass Merlin Golf Course; take the next left turn and follow the road back to St Eval church and the car park.

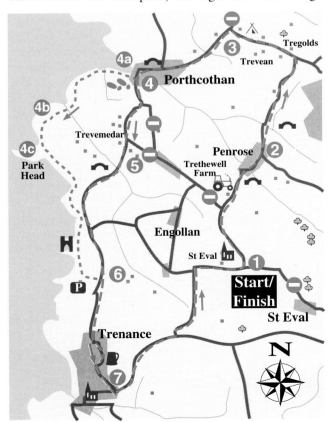

FACT FILE

Distance 9 or 10 miles
Time 3–4 hours
Map OS Landranger 200
Start/parking St Eval parish church, grid ref 872692
Terrain Some steep descents and ascents. Avoid coast path in heavy rain or high winds
Nearest towns Wadebridge, Padstow and St Columb
Refreshments Tredrea Inn at Porthcothan, Bedruthan House café and Carnewas Cliff café
Public transport Western National (no 53). BR Par to Newquay
Stiles None
Suitable for Older children, dogs on leads

ALONG THE WAY

Enjoy some glorious North Cornwall coast walking and some spectacular countryside as you walk from St Eval parish church. There is a short but worthwhile diversion to view Carnewas Cliff (the well-known Bedruthan Steps) and the cliff staircase. The church is always open and welcomes visitors. The tower was restored in the 16th century by the Merchant Venturers of Bristol as a navigation aid for their sea captains sailing up the Bristol Channel. The church is well worth visiting as it contains much of interest, including many Royal Air Force memorials of the Second World War.

Take the coast path option to visit the dramatic Bedruthan Steps

MYSTERIOUS MOORS

Experience the rewards of peaceful moors, breathtaking coastal scenery and an abundance of wildlife on this challenging circular walk.

1 Take the wide track opposite Men-an-Tol Studio for about ½ mile. Turn right over the stile (signed Men-an-Tol Ancient Monument) and continue along a grass ride to the stones. Pass the stones on the right and go straight ahead towards the mine standing on the skyline. Descend the shallow valley and when the track divides bear right. Cross a stream and walk straight uphill. Pass a mine on your right and continue to a T junction.

2 Turn left and stay on the track. Past the cottages the track bears right and emerges on to a very narrow road. Turn left and walk down the road to the hamlet of Tredinnick. At the bend, when the road continues right, turn left on a No Through Road signed Bodrify. Stay on the road, which peters into a track.

3 Pass through the gateway and in about 50yds take a track to the right over a low stone wall past Bodriffy ancient settlement. Take this track. Although it bends slightly it runs in an almost straight line up over the moor to a minor road.

4 At the road turn left, following the sign for Gurnard's Head. When this road meets the main B3306 turn left and continue ahead to the Gurnard's Head Hotel. Passing the hotel on your left, walk down to the last isolated house. At the bottom corner of the garden wall, near a mine building, turn left on to the coastal footpath.

5 Continue along the coastal footpath, taking great care over the huge boulders as you climb Bosigran. There is a sheer drop over cliffs on the other side.

6 When the cliffs appear straight for a distance ahead, look for a low neat granite stone wall on your left, then head inland beside it. Head up the track, over a stile to the right of a gate. Cross the next stile and emerge at the road, which you cross.

7 Almost immediately turn left up a public bridleway which climbs Watch Croft. Pass a mine building and granite house on your right, and go straight down to the road. Turn left down the road to return to the start.

FACT FILE

Distance 10½ miles
Time 5–6 hours
Map OS Landranger 203
Start/parking Opposite Men-an-Tol Studio (ample parking), grid ref 419344
Terrain Moderate over moors, some difficult climbs along coast
Nearest town Penzance
Refreshments Gurnard's Head Hotel at Treen
Public transport Bus from Penzance
Stiles Nine, all easy
Suitable for Older children

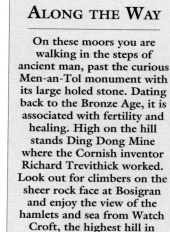

ALONG THE WAY

On these moors you are walking in the steps of ancient man, past the curious Men-an-Tol monument with its large holed stone. Dating back to the Bronze Age, it is associated with fertility and healing. High on the hill stands Ding Dong Mine where the Cornish inventor Richard Trevithick worked. Look out for climbers on the sheer rock face at Bosigran and enjoy the view of the hamlets and sea from Watch Croft, the highest hill in Penwith at 827ft.

Crawling through the Men-an-Tol was said to cure rheumatism and rickets

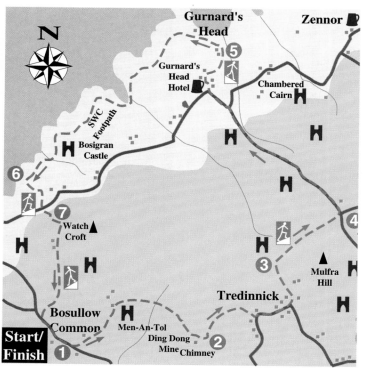

THE WILD WEST

Enjoy this circular walk in one of the wildest regions of west Cornwall offering excellent views from Woon Gumpus Common and the rugged beauty of the coast.

1 Walk up St John's Terrace at the side of the car park. This narrow road soon becomes a track, passes a small wood and emerges on to the B3318 road. Turn right, continue along the road until you reach a minor road on the right and a small layby on the left.

2 Turn left across the layby on to a track over Woon Gumpus Common, marked 'Permissive Path'. Head in a straight line towards Chûn Quoit, which looks like a large mushroom in the skyline. The path has periodic marker posts.

3 At the Quoit bear right for Chûn Castle, then return to the Quoit. A few paces before it, to the right, take the narrow track downhill. At the wide farm track turn left and continue to a stone stile and marker post on the left before the large wooden barn.

4 Over the stile the path now continues across four small fields all accessed by stiles, each one visible from the last.

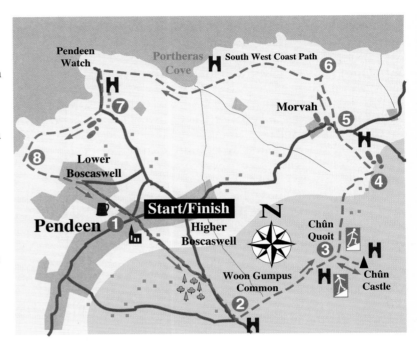

5 Cross the road and walk straight ahead towards the sign for Morvah and the church. Turn right over the stile just before the church. Follow the lane to a low stone wall with a stream to the left. Over the wall continue for about 100yds.

6 Turn left along the coastal footpath. The path descends into the valley behind Portheras Cove. Cross the river on stepping stones and continue to Pendeen Watch lighthouse. Walk up the road to a row of terraced houses on the left.

7 On the right directly opposite the last house ('Enys', no. 6) is a low granite milestone marked Cape Cornwall 3½ miles. Turn right here and rejoin the coastal footpath. The path winds down the narrow valley with a stream on the left. At the next coastal footpath marker cross the stream and walk up and over the headland.

8 As the path heads inland bear left at the next sign. Don't cross the new footbridge. Continue with mine workings on the right. When the track meets the road take the right fork and continue straight ahead on the road to the corner shop. The bus stop and car park are on the opposite side of the road.

FACT FILE

Distance 7 miles
Time 3 hours
Map OS Landranger 203
Start/parking Pendeen village car park, grid ref 383344
Terrain Easy. Moderate hill climbs. Some areas muddy after rain
Nearest town Penzance
Refreshments Various at Pendeen. None on route
Public transport Bus from Penzance to St Just stops at car park in Pendeen, Monday–Saturday
Stiles Many, stone or wood, all easy
Suitable for Older children, dogs on leads

ALONG THE WAY

This part of Cornwall is rich in archaeological antiquities and two are passed on this walk. Chûn Castle, a hillfort of drystone ramparts, was built before 200BC. Its staggered entrance looks west towards Chûn Quoit. Quoits are thought to have been chambered tombs and this one stands intact. Until recently parts of a wreck could be seen at Portheras Cove. A sign above the beach warns of the danger of bathing or walking barefoot here because of it.

A Day on the Island

Take a day trip by helicopter to Tresco and enjoy a coastal and inland walk around the island, visiting the unique sub-tropical Abbey Gardens.

1 From the heliport walk towards the sea and join the road which skirts Appletree Bay before climbing Plumb Hill. From here there is a splendid view of the Islands of Samson, Gugh, St Agnes and Annet with the Western Rocks away to the south-west.

2 The road now continues, with the Great Pool on your right, to New Grimsby where there is a craft shop, art gallery and a small café on the quayside. Across the water is Bryher, which has a lovely sandy beach.

3 Walk past the quay and carry on up the hill. Go along the road which skirts the coast, passing Frenchman's Point, to Cromwell's Castle and then around the top of the island to Gun Hill and Piper's Hole. Skirting Gimble Porth, Gimble Point and Merchant's Point, the road reaches the Island Hotel.

4 At Old Grimsby turn right and follow the road uphill after passing the Island School and St Nicholas Church. Descending Towns Hill you pass the post office and the New Inn before coming back to New Grimsby.

5 Retrace your steps for a short distance and then turn left by Great Pool. Follow the track known as Racket Town Lane. Ignore the turning to the right, bear left and descend for a short distance to take the next right turning with the old Block House clearly in view.

6 Now follow this sandy path past Rushy Point, Rushy Porth, Lizard Point and Pentle Bay, enjoying excellent views first of Round Island, then St Martin's, the Eastern Isles and St Mary's.

7 The path then joins the grandly named Penzance Road, which is really little more than a track down to Pentle Bay. The clearly signed right turn takes you to the entrance to the famous Abbey Gardens.

8 Within the gardens there are many paths and terraces where you can admire the profusion of sub-tropical trees, shrubs, plants and flowers. Make time, too, to visit Valhalla, a museum containing the figureheads of ships wrecked off the Islands. The heliport's Terminal 1 can easily be reached from inside the Abbey Gardens; allow 20 minutes pre-boarding time for the return flight to Penzance.

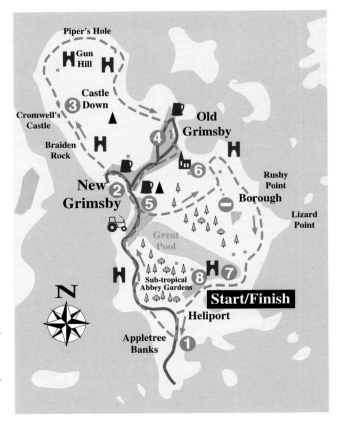

Fact File

Distance 6 miles
Time 2½ hours, plus extra time for sightseeing and a visit to the gardens
Map OS Landranger 203
Start Tresco Heliport, grid ref 894140
Parking At Penzance Heliport, Eastern Green, clearly signed off the A30
Terrain Gently undulating throughout
Nearest towns Penzance (mainland); Hugh Town, St Mary's
Refreshments A choice of restaurants, cafés, pubs and hotels in Penzance. On Tresco the New Inn, Quayside Café at New Grimsby, the Island Hotel (Old Grimsby) and at the Abbey Gardens

Public Transport British International Helicopters – three flights on weekdays departing Penzance 10.50am and Tresco 4.10pm. No service on Sundays. Flight reservations should be made as far in advance as possible, tel 01736 63871
Stiles None
Suitable for Wheelchairs, but difficulties could be experienced boarding the helicopter. Enquiries should be made before making reservations – tel 01736 63871. Folding buggies and pushchairs present no problem. Small dogs are carried on the helicopter (subject to advance arrangements) and dogs are allowed on Tresco but must be kept on a lead in the Abbey Gardens

ALONG THE WAY

Tresco, the second largest of the Isles of Scilly, can be reached direct by a British International Sikorsky helicopter operating a regular, all-year-round service from Penzance Heliport.
The helicopter service gives you five hours on the island, which you need to complete the walk and visit the Abbey Gardens.
Penzance is also the terminus of the railway line from Plymouth where main line routes including those from London Paddington, South Wales, the Midlands, the North of England and Scotland converge.
There are no motor vehicles on Tresco other than tractors and those owned and operated by the Tresco Estate, but self-drive electric battery-cars (seating four people) are available by prior arrangement and when available the Estate passenger trailers will pick up those wishing to ride.

ANCIENT LAND

Walk round the largest of the Isles of Scilly, past a wealth of ancient sites.

1 Start at Hugh Town. A shuttle service operates from the airport and the main street is a short distance from the quay. Take the right-hand fork past the park, up to the church and fork right again.

2 This paths leads to Porth Cressa; skirt the bay and follow the coast path to the headland. The lighthouse is a prominent man-made feature, while the natural granite has been weathered into surrealistic shapes.

3 From Pulpit Rock you can look directly into Old Town Bay and across the water to the airport. The path continues along

the shore and you soon reach Old Town Church and its peaceful churchyard, where Lord Wilson is buried.

4 From Old Town, once the chief port and town of Scilly, take the narrow road along the sea edge, which becomes a path along the coastline. This takes you past the airport, towards Porth Hellick Bay.

5 Leave the freshwater pond on your left and take the path around the coastline, going through the gate at the eastern end. Follow the path uphill (note the signpost pointing to the ancient passage grave). At this point you can take a short-cut back to Hugh Town by road. Otherwise, continue along the coastal footpath to Pelistry Bay (where there is another short-cut back to Hugh Town, via Holy Vale).

6 Leaving Pelistry Bay, follow the well-defined coast path northwards over Tolls Hill, enjoying the fine views of St Martin's and the Eastern Isles. There are several more ancient burial chambers here, dating from 1500–1000 BC. The path continues up to Bar Point with Telegraph Tower clearly visible.

7 From Bar Point follow the path past the remains of another ancient village to descend into Hugh Town with a fine view of Tresco and Bryher, to complete the main walk.

8 If time permits, and you want to complete the Island walk, take the road westwards towards Star Castle and from there to the Garrison. Turn right and from the path you can see Annet, Gugh and St Agnes. Finish the walk in an anti-clockwise direction, still following the clearly defined path which finally overlooks Porth Cressa Bay and brings you back to Hugh Town.

Map labels

N

Bar Point

Ancient Village
Telegraph Tower
Toll's Island
Pelistry Bay
Toll Hill
Porthloo
Alternative Route
Holy Vale
Ferry Quay
Star Castle
Hugh Town
Alternative Route
Airport
Old Town
Start/Finish
Porth Hellick Bay
The Garrison
Porth Cressa
Old Town Bay
Newfoundland Rocks
Lighthouse
Peninnis Headland

FACT FILE

Distance 7½ miles, plus an extra 1½ miles around the Garrison
Time 4½ or 5¼ hours
Map OS Landranger 203
Start Hugh Town, St Mary's, grid ref 902110
Parking At the main seafront car park in Penzance (10 minutes' walk from Lighthouse Pier) if crossing by sea; or Penzance Heliport or Land's End Airport
Terrain Gently undulating throughout
Nearest towns Penzance (mainland); Hugh Town
Refreshments A choice of restaurants, cafés and pubs in Penzance and on St Mary's
Public transport RMS *Scillonian III* sails at 9.15am daily Monday–

Saturday, April to October from Lighthouse Pier, returns from St Mary's at 4.30pm. For times and fares information, tel 01736 62009. Skybus services operate throughout the year from Land's End Airport and from Bristol, Exeter, Newquay and Plymouth. Skyrail-Intercity and other inclusive packages are also available, tel 01736 787017. British International Helicopters operate 12 flights on weekdays; flight reservations should be made as far in advance as possible. Tel 01736 63871
Stiles None
Suitable for Children and dogs

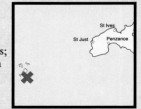

ALONG THE WAY

St Mary's is the main island in this group, but the absence of cars (visitors are not allowed to bring them) means that it has retained its peace and tranquillity – features that attracted the former prime minister Lord Wilson to the island. Like all the islands, it is graced with a temperate climate, making it ideal for early flower growing, and has a vast array of Bronze Age remains, some of which you pass on this route.

The shorter walks are designed for those with limited time on a day trip; the sea crossing only allows about 4½ hours on St Mary's (the ship's whistle reverberates throughout the islands 30 minutes before the 4.30pm departure time). Please be aware that timings are tight and some walkers may wish to opt for the shorter routes back.

This ancient village on Halangy Down is one of several historic sites on St Mary's

COASTAL ROADS

Cross Carrick Roads and the River Fal by ferry during this coastal and woodland walk which can be started at one of two points.

1 Leaving the quayside car park, turn right and follow Falmouth's usually bustling main street as far as the Prince of Wales Pier.

2 At the pier you embark on the St Mawes ferry (frequent, well-advertised sailing times) for the 30–35 minute crossing.

3 Disembark at St Mawes and turn left along the waterside street. Follow this for ½ mile until you reach St Mawes Castle.

4 After exploring the castle turn left up the fairly steep hill (signed A3078 – St Just Lane). At the T junction at the top of the hill turn left. In 1 mile, at Tregear Vean, note the finger-post to St Just (1 mile). This is for the adventurous, as it can be very muddy. The path continues just inside the hedge for about ½ mile then rejoins the A3078.

5 St Just Lane is a cluster of houses at a crossroads. If you decide to visit the church, turn left following signs down to St Just Church and Bar.

6 After you have visited the church retrace your steps to St Just Lane and turn left on to the B3289.

7 At this road junction ignore the road to Tolverne and bear left. Continue on the main road that leads to the King Harry Ferry.

8 Here embark on the ferry for the short river crossing to the Feock side beneath Trelissick.

9 When you disembark walk up the steep hill to the entrance to Trelissick, keeping a wary eye out for cars. Here is the car park from which you can also begin this walk (in reverse) ending at either St Mawes or, if you wish, at Falmouth, to explore the interesting old seaport.

10 The well-signed 2½ mile long Woodland Walk takes you down to the riverside and along by a picturesque creek, before the fairly steep ascent to road level once again. If you have started from Falmouth, after perhaps taking refreshment or even visiting the well-known National Trust Trelissick Gardens, walk down the hill to board the King Harry Ferry and retrace your route back to St Just Lane (5) and St Mawes (3) to take the next ferry back to Prince of Wales pier at Falmouth (2).

NB It is not now possible to complete what was known as the circular Ferries Walk, the passenger (rowing boat) ferry across Restronguet Creek having ceased to operate.

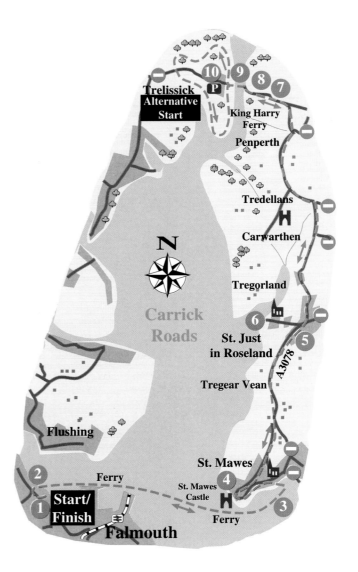

Distance 12 miles (including the diversion to St Just in Roseland Church) or 14½ miles (including the Trelissick Woodland Walk)
Time 4½–5 hours (excluding waiting time for ferries)
Map OS Landranger 204
Starts/parking Falmouth Town Centre (Church Street) Quayside car park, grid ref 810325; or Trelissick (NT) car park, grid ref 835397
Terrain Undulating with a few steep but short slopes. Good road surfaces; woodland walk can be muddy after rain
Nearest towns Falmouth, Truro, St Mawes
Refreshments A variety of restaurants and inns at Falmouth and St Mawes. Usual NT fare at Trelissick
Public transport Falmouth is well served by bus and branch line train services
Stiles None
Suitable for Older children and well controlled dogs.

The Woodland Walk at Trelissick takes you alongside the River Fal

COASTAL GEMS

This circular walk in Mount Edgcumbe Country Park has several spectacular optional extras.

1 The walk begins at the Cremyll Lodge Visitor Centre just inside the clearly signed entrance to the Country Park and either follows the main drive to Mount Edgcumbe House or (1a) follows the path immediately to the left inside the main gates towards the Orangery and the formal gardens.

1a Follow any of the paths in and around the splendid formal gardens, or the direct path following the sea wall towards the Garden Battery and continue past the Amphitheatre, Milton's Temple and up the steep slope to the Folly. You will soon join the path from point 3.

2 Take the main drive, keep to the right and follow the roadway uphill past the pond, leaving the house on your left. Take the right fork leading to the car park entrance, then the left-hand sloping path through the wood. At the top go through the deer fence gate (please close all gates) and follow the path towards Maker Church.

3 At the end of this path go through gateway leading into Maker car park and, keeping parallel with the fence, walk south towards the open sea and a gate. At the bottom corner of the fence continue down the slope and follow the track round to its lowest point to take the sharp right turn down to the centre of Hooe Lake Valley.

4 The path then goes steeply down parallel with the fence to a stile adjoining the road. Bear right and pass in front of Hooe Lake Cottage. On the left, opposite the cottage, climb over the stile and follow the path around through a dense copse.

5 Keep to this path and in a few hundred yards to your left, pass the entrance to a footpath which gives access to Sandway Point and the beach.

6 Follow the main path towards Kingsand; the land rises to over 400ft above sea level just beyond the now disused Grenville Battery which dominates the skyline. Pass through the gate, turn sharp right almost opposite Lower Row and on to Devonport Hill.

7 Follow the streets through Kingsand and Cawsand to pick up the well-signed coastal footpath for the next mile of undulating path.

7a The path leads directly to Penlee Point, from which the views across to Rame Head are superb. Return to Cawsand by way of the well-defined road and then into adjacent Kingsand.

7b Should you wish to extend your walk still further, follow the undulating (at times steep) section of the South West Coast Path to Rame Head, returning to Cawsand and Kingsand either by the same path or around Rame village and church by the well-signed network of country roads.

8 Once again on the footpath by which you entered Kingsand from the Country Park, look for the iron railings which form the boundary of Maker Battery. Follow the path through the copse as it rises to level ground, passing the remains of an ancient covered well on the left. This path joins the road from Kingsand. Turn right and follow the road around the back of Maker Farm.

9 Take the right-hand bend (signed Fort Picklecombe) and follow the road for about 100yds to the public footpath sign, climb over the low rail and cross the field following the line of electricity poles to another rail. Beyond this is a field with a third stile; ahead is Friary Mano. The stile leads on to a concreted drive; cross the drive into the lane opposite and after passing through another gate, follow the path as it makes its way back on to the field adjoining Maker Church and car park. Return to the main gate (Cremyll Lodge) by way of Drywalk Wood and the Avenue.

Plymouth Sound viewed from Mount Edgcumbe Park

ALONG THE WAY

Approaching from any direction the views in this area are superb, especially across the Hamoaze and upriver, with the Dartmoor Tors for backdrop and the city of Plymouth in the foreground.
Mount Edgcumbe House is open to the public and is well worth a visit if time permits. Originally built in the mid-16th century, it has undergone many changes, including rebuilding earlier this century.

SHORT BUT STEEP

Tackle this short walk after lunch at the excellent Dolphin Inn in Kingston. The strenuous ups and downs will certainly ensure your meal is fully digested.

1 From the Dolphin Inn go past the church and at the next junction (Wonwell Gate) turn right for Wonwell beach. After ¼ mile a stile takes you into a field on your left, from which you have lovely views down to the River Erme in front of you and to Dartmoor on your right. Follow the left-hand field edge through the gate into the next field and keep on against the same left-hand hedge until it veers off to the left. Bear slightly right and carry on towards the trees. Cross the stile on to a path between two hedges.

2 The way is quite obvious, and takes you over two further stiles and above the buildings of Torr Down Farm which you can see below you on your right. Eventually another stile takes you into a wood, and you follow the top edge. The path then starts to descend fairly steeply and when you come to an obvious junction by a ditch and bank, follow the ditch downhill until you reach a metalled road. Go left towards Wonwell Beach, one of the most beautiful in the area.

3 Beyond the traffic bollards, and just before you reach the beach, a signpost and some steps direct you up on to the coast path which runs through the wood then just above the cliffs. It descends and skirts across the head of Fernycombe Beach before another stile takes you back on to the cliffs that lead to Beacon Point.

4 Between Beacon Point and Westcombe Beach the path follows the cliffs, sometimes squeezed to the edge by a fence. Take care close to Beacon Point, especially with dogs or children because the cliffs are crumbly and the path is close to the drop. Further along you will encounter several steep descents and ascents. Steps have been built in places to make walking easier, but the height of the risers ensures maximum effort for leg and heart muscles.

5 You descend a winding, stepped path and cross a stile to Westcombe Beach, an excellent spot to stop and cool down

and perhaps have a swim. Before the bridge across the brook take the permissive footpath to Kingston. This leads up the valley to your left, following the west bank of the brook.

6 When you come to the wooden footbridge, cross the brook through a coppice of felled trees and on the other side of this go over the stile and turn right on to the track. About 100yds further up is a five-barred gate and stile, where the track forks. Either route will take you back to Kingston, but the right-hand route is the prettier of the two, following the valley past Okenbury Farm. The brook has been dammed all the way along here to form a series of ponds which are rich in bird life. You soon pass the Kingston Water Treatment Works on your right, and shortly after this you come to a tarmac road with a white cottage. Turn left and climb the hill. At the next junction turn right, then first left which takes you back to the Dolphin Inn.

FACT FILE

Distance 5 miles
Time 2½–3 hours
Map OS Landranger 202
Start The Dolphin Inn, Kingston, grid ref 635477
Parking Limited by the church, otherwise by the sides of the road in the village
Terrain Footpaths, tracks and lanes. Some extremely strenuous climbs

Nearest town Ivybridge
Refreshments The Dolphin Inn, Kingston
Public transport Limited daily service from Ivybridge, and on Fridays only from Plymouth. Tel 01752 222666
Stiles Eleven, all easy
Suitable for Most fit people, dogs on leads, especially near cliffs

A tranquil spot on the estuary of the River Erme, near Wonwell

ALONG THE WAY

For those who relish dramatic cliff scenery this route is the ideal choice. The Dartmouth slates, once quarried for roofing stone, rise in huge unbroken slabs on which the sun sometimes gleams as if they were enormous mirrors. Beacon Point itself is an interloper, a spur of sandstone with quite different characteristics, where the cliff edge crumbles and flakes off into the sea. Inland from Westcombe beach the path passes through an ancient withy bed, once harvested for making crab pots and baskets. The Heritage Coast Service is now working in conjunction with the owner and a local basketmaker to restore the site to its traditional use.

CREEKS AND BRIDGES

Enjoy different aspects of the Kingsbridge estuary and its creeks.

1 From the start, return to the main road and go west for 200yds beyond the Globe Inn. Now turn left on to the footpath which takes you through a gate, then diagonally right through the field. In the opposite corner, stone steps lead you on to a path that runs above the house and parallel to the creek.

2 By the barn at Clevehouse, cross the stream at the head of the creek and continue following the creek south-west. Cross a number of stiles into fields, some with dog gates, until the path passes through uncultivated ground, through a thicket and down on to the foreshore. Follow this for about 250yds to where the signed footpath winds away from the creek and up through a wood. You soon come to a metalled road. Follow this north to the first sharp right-hand bend and a footpath sign.

3 Go through the gate and across the field. This path may not be obvious if ploughing has just taken place, but if you make straight for the nearest white house in West Charleton you will be going in the right direction. Turn left at the fence, and 100yds further on, cross two stiles into a meadow. Cross this, leaving the duckpond on your right. A gate to the right of the white picket fence leads on to a short track and then to the main road. Turn left.

4 Go past the Ashburton Arms. After 500yds, take the road past the church, and take the footpath through the second gate into the field. Skirt the southern and western edges of this, and enter the next field through a gate in the north-west corner.

5 Follow the fenceline north. In the north-east corner of the field is a stile in the wall. Descend the steep hill to a spring. Now the path leads diagonally to a gate in the north-west corner of the field close to the creek. It then runs parallel to the river to another stile a few yards before a footbridge that crosses the creek.

6 If you want to shorten the walk by ½ mile, don't cross the stile, climb steeply uphill parallel to the hedge until you emerge on to a lane. Carry on uphill, cross over at Duncombe Cross and this muddy green lane takes you all the way back to Frogmore.

7 Alternatively, cross the stile and continue to the bridge. A second stile, partially hidden behind a tree, takes you into the next field. Follow the river up and you will see Bowcombe cottage in front of you, effectively barring the way. You will have to climb uphill above the cottage to the gate that takes you into the lane. Turn right. You are now on the green lane to Frogmore.

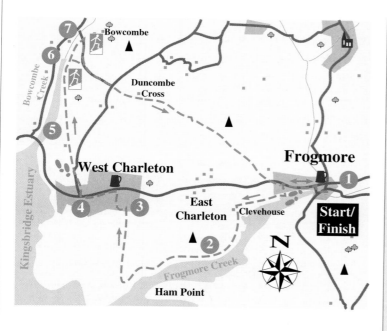

FACT FILE

Distance 5¾ or 6¼ miles
Time 2–3 hours
Maps OS Landranger 202
Start/parking Over the bridge in Frogmore village, grid ref 776425
Terrain Easy paths and green lanes. Muddy. Check tide times. The foreshore stretch on Frogmore Creek can be covered at high spring tides
Nearest Town Kingsbridge
Refreshments Globe Inn, Frogmore, Ashburton Arms, West Charleton
Public transport 93 bus runs about six times daily between Dartmouth and Kingsbridge. Ring Western National, Plymouth 01752 222666
Stiles Numerous
Suitable for Children, dogs on leads

ALONG THE WAY

The Kingsbridge estuary is a ria or drowned river valley, although there is no river – all that flows into it are small streams. Bowcombe Creek is spanned by two bridges, and there is another pre-17th-century bridge spanning the stream just below Bowcombe cottage. The lowest bridge, carrying the main Kingsbridge to Dartmouth road, was built in 1831.

LIST OF CONTRIBUTORS

Maps by Jeremy Ashcroft

Jan Barwick (South West): Short but Steep;
Creeks and Bridges

Brian Beadle (Yorkshire, Humberside and the North West):
Past Reflections

James Carron (Scotland): Heather and Hauntings;
Skye Walking; Circle in the Sand; On the Beach;
Harbouring a Scenic Treasure

Nick Channer (South East): Gateway to the World;
Power of the Wind; A Medieval Pepper Pot

Martin Collins (Wales): Coastal Heritage

Barry Crawshaw (Scotland): Fairies in the Woods;
Forest and Firths; Ever Green

Paddy Dillon (North and Ireland): Through the Wild Glen;
Round the Sound; A Poet's Tower; St Assicus' League;
Coast Line

Slyvie Dobson (South East): Head for Heights;
Power and Glory

John Fenna (Wales): A Different Angle; Burials and
Invasions; In the Footsteps of the Welsh Saints;
Cliffs, Birds and Beaches

Jack French (Lincolnshire and East Anglia): Views from the
Castle; On the Wing

Debbie Hamilton (Wales): Sand and Castles;
Shaped by the Sea

Brian Hollman (Lincolnshire and East Anglia): Sea Breezes

Dewi Jones (Wales): Holy Island; Lover's Island;
Castles and Coast; Coastal Heritage; Where the Sand Whistles

Tim Knight (South West): Poet's Paradise

Margaret McManners (North): Rocks, Sand and Sea at
Bamburgh; Kittiwakes and Kippers at Craster

Laurence Main (Wales): Coastal Inspiration

Julie Meech (South West):Beside the Severn Sea

Carole Nadin (Lincolnshire and East Anglia): Sea and Sky;
Winter Refuge

Ivan Rabey (South West): Church and Coast; A Day on the
Island; Ancient Land; Coastal Roads; Coastal Gems

David Robertson (Scotland): Hidden Treasure

Jason Smalley (Yorkshire, Humberside and the North West):
Village by the Sea

Nigel Vile (South West): A Lost Dallas

Mary Welsh (Scotland, Yorkshire, Humberside and The
North West): Nature's Clowns and Pirates; Bird Island;
Double Adventure; Northern Delights; Natural History;
Island Heritage; Glories of Lewis; To the Lighthouse; The
Giant's Island; Paradise Island; On the Rocks; Rocky Island;
Island Treasures; (The North): Roman Remains; High
Drama; From Abbey to Artists; Cliffs and Railways; Coastal
Relics; Circular Walk from Pilling Marsh

Maggie Weston (South West): Coast and River; Mysterious
Moors; The Wild West

Further photographs contributed by:

Maureen Fleming: page 91, 11, 15
Derek Forss: page 30
Alan Bedding: page 67
Welsh Tourist Board: page 75
Rupert Clegg: page 107
IWTO/Peter Titmus: page 103, 105
Roy Westlake: page 125
Martin Johnson: page 119
Stephen Power: page 65
David Hughes: page 63